Previous page:
Stepping out into the new world of the nationalised British Railways is 'Merchant Navy' class 4-6-2 No 35015 *Rotterdam Lloyd* at the head of a West of England train leaving Waterloo. The locomotive is in the early BR standard blue livery for top link express engines, and the first coach carries carmine red and cream colours. *BR*

Below:
Stanier 'Duchess' Pacific No 46238 *City of Carlisle* in gleaming BR crimson lake livery is seen leaving Penrith on 15 February 1964 with a football special to Preston. Of interest is the leading pair of coaches, an ex-LNER articulated twin. All the coaches were in the standard lined maroon livery which was slightly darker than the locomotive's shade. *Peter J. Robinson*

Left:
The first BR lion and wheel totem, designed by Abram Games for the British Transport Commission in 1949.
Sam Lambert

RAILWAY LIVERIES

BR STEAM 1948-1968

BRIAN HARESNAPE

revised by **COLIN BOOCOCK**

LONDON

IAN ALLAN LTD

Dedication

This book was the brainchild of Brian Haresnape. His original manuscript was with the publisher at the time of Brian's unexpected and tragic death in Spain in 1987.

It was my pleasure to meet Brian on a number of occasions, as professionals (me as a railwayman and he as a graphic designer), and in more informal circumstances as enthusiasts. I shall remember his charm, his skill as a designer and his warmth. His prowess as an author is well known. I can only hope that the work I have been asked to do to enlarge the size and scope of this book will do Brian the justice he deserves.

I therefore humbly dedicate this book to the memory of Brian Haresnape.

Colin Boocock

Opinions

The original manuscript of this book on the design of railway liveries was written by a designer. Any opinions expressed on BR liveries in this book are those of the author, Brian Haresnape, unless specifically stated otherwise.

Colin Boocock
Editor

CONTENTS

Front cover:
'Jubilee' class 4-6-0 No 45694 *Bellerophon* is seen at St Pancras in experimental green livery.
From a painting by George Heiron

First published 1989
Reprinted 1993

ISBN 0 7110 1856 1

Published by Ian Allan Ltd, Shepperton, Surrey; and printed in Great Britain by Ian Allan Printing Ltd, Coombelands House, Addlestone, Surrey KT15 1HY.

INTRODUCTION

All Change!

New Year's Day 1948 has gone down in railway history as the day the government nationalised the British railway system, effectively grouping the Big Four private companies into one huge and unwieldy whole. In fact, the new British Railways as it was called, was formed of six Regions. New boundaries were created that in some areas cut across established company territories, particularly in Scotland which was henceforth served by one, eventually homogeneous, Region. Otherwise the Regions were allied to the former railways, except that the London & North Eastern Railway in England was split between the Eastern and North Eastern Regions.

Below:
Something of a shock to the eyes in 1948 was the very bright and 'acid' apple green colour tried out on some 4-6-0s. This was considerably brighter than the usual LNER apple green shade. Lining out was in LNWR style. The 'Jubilee' class 4-6-0 No 45694 *Bellerophon* is seen at St Pancras station about to leave with the 4.50pm down Bradford restaurant car express on 25 August 1948. All the carriages had been experimentally painted chocolate and cream.
E. D. Bruton

The nationalisation also absorbed smaller companies such as the Mersey Railway, the Cheshire Lines Committee, the East Kent Railway and the Kent & East Sussex Railway.

Staff loyalties were stretched in many districts, but this is not a political treatise and I must not enter into the pros and cons of nationalisation versus privatisation. This book is concerned with the first two decades of British Railways, 1948 to 1968, the full span of the life of standard gauge steam traction on BR, and the steam locomotive and hauled carriage liveries that evolved during that period.

These years marked the final era when steam traction was dominant on BR. It is intended that a later book will cover the liveries applied to electric and diesel locomotives and multiple-units.

Under the 1947 Transport Act the British Transport Commission was set up and included in its sphere of actions the following:

- The Railway Executive (to manage British Railways)
- The London Transport Executive
- Docks and Inland Waterways
- British Road Services and Pickfords
- The Tilling bus group

Above:

A Stanier 'Black 5' becomes a 'Green 5'! This is brand-new No M4764, painted experimentally in GWR green with orange and black lining in January 1948. Two others received LNER and SR green liveries and all three took part in the display to BTC officers at Addison Road station for comparison. No decision was reached! *P. Ransome-Wallis*

The Railway Executive not only had the railways under its control, it also was given the ancillary railway businesses, the docks, hotels, steamships and road cartage. The six railway Regions were:

- Eastern Region, formed of routes south of Doncaster (inclusive) of the former London & North Eastern Railway (LNER)
- London Midland Region, comprising routes in England operated by the former London,

- Midland & Scottish Railway (LMS)
- North Eastern Region, formed of LNER routes north of Doncaster (exclusive) and south of the Scottish border
- Scottish Region, being all railways in Scotland, both LNER and LMS
- Southern Region, which broadly consisted of the lines of the former Southern Railway (SR)
- Western Region, the routes of the former Great Western Railway (GWR)

For stations and elsewhere, new base colours were decided upon. These colours were: maroon for the London Midland Region (LMR); chocolate brown for the Western Region (WR); malachite green for the Southern Region; ultramarine blue for the Eastern Region (ER); light Caledonian blue for the Scottish

Region (ScR) and tangerine orange for the North Eastern Region (NER).

The Inherited Liveries

The newly-created Railway Executive was quick off the mark in considering new liveries for its 20,000 locomotives and its vast fleet of rolling stock. But before commencing that story it is worthwhile taking a brief look at the state-of-the-art at the time of the national takeover, which was a mere three years after the end of World War 2 when Britain was still enduring a period of considerable austerity.

Wartime had seen the majority of British locomotives painted black, although some survived the whole period carrying their prewar colours (scarcely visible under successive layers of grime, it must be said!). The passenger carriages had suffered in similar fashion although some colour was retained minus the lining out and fine varnish finishes of prewar days. Freight stock was notable for a lack of paint, wooden wagons being left unpainted when repaired, and others being merely touched up, mostly in grey. Lack of cleaners (although women were recruited) meant that the general standards of day-to-day presentation had seriously declined, although certain areas of the country did manage to retain presentable rolling stock, mostly away from the larger cities.

Each of the Big Four reviewed the livery situation once peace was restored to the nation, and each had actually begun to implement new schemes when the shadow of the forthcoming nationalisation was cast upon them, even before most had really got under way. Taking each of the four railways in turn it is evident that — given more time — some of the prewar finery would have been restored, except in the case of the LMS.

The LNER had announced in 1946 an ambitious plan to repaint all its locomotives in apple green, and to retain a varnished teak finish for its passenger carriages (despite the newest ones being of all-steel construction!). It had got under way with this scheme in 1947. One prior experiment (see *Railway Liveries: 1923-1947*, by the author) was made with the deep blue of the former Great Eastern Railway, and one welcome deviation from green was the use of the prewar garter blue for the streamlined Gresley Pacifics.

The Southern Railway, under O. V. S. Bulleid's guiding hand, applied malachite green, using yellow and black bordering on conventional

Left:
While the Regions waited for decisions on colours to be made, they continued to paint locomotives in the styles of the former companies, right through 1948. Prefixes to the engine numbers indicated the former owning railways. Class S15 4-6-0 No s838 heads a down goods train near Winchfield, Hampshire on 20 April 1948. The engine has BRITISH RAILWAYS on its tender in full SR 'sunshine' lettering, setting off its otherwise dull plain black livery.
Lens of Sutton/E. C. Griffith

locomotives, and three broad yellow bands on Bulleid Pacifics. The GWR started a return to traditional Brunswick green for locomotives, and chocolate and cream for carriages. The LMS, after some half-hearted experiments with maroon and a deep blue-grey colour for locomotives, had decided upon the course of least resistance and had embarked upon a new livery of black, with some maroon and straw lining for the more important locomotives only. Carriages were in a maroon shade with minimal lining out. On all four railways, many locomotives retained their wartime black, being merely retouched as necessary as they passed through the workshops for repair, and a similar 'make do and mend' policy was applied to many carriages and wagons.

Shortages of paint, and problems of rising costs, went against a rapid repaint of the war-scarred railway fleets, and in any case there still was a chronic shortage of cleaners. Weary men returning from war service did not seem too anxious to take on the grime and long hours of railway work, so characteristic of the period. It must be remembered that nearly all cleaning was done by hand, and the era of automatic washing plants and other mechanical aids was in its infancy in Britain.

Cleaning a large steam locomotive by hand was a lengthy process, carried out in the open air or in smoke-filled sheds. Cleaning was traditionally considered as a form of apprenticeship for the footplate grades, as a first rung of the ladder towards becoming a locomotive fireman and eventually a driver. It had the advantage that a young cleaner got used to, and understood, the working parts of a locomotive; it was however very poorly paid work and many left during this period of their career for alternative and cleaner jobs.

Likewise carriage cleaning was very laborious and undertaken in poor working conditions and at odd hours of the day and night. It is not an exaggeration to say that the steam railway environment of 1945 to 1948 was the worst ever in the history of our railways. The author well recalls journeys undertaken with his mother on various outings when she would express her horror at the filthy carriage in which we had to travel! The rare and splendid sight of a clean locomotive remained in my mind's eye for months afterwards, so accustomed had we become to dirt as an integral part of rail travel.

Early BR Liveries

By the summer of 1947 the Big Four were pulling themselves together. Given time, each would have restored its identity and pride, but political events were to halt this progress. On 31 December 1947 they were all thrown into the state melting pot, and emerged next day as British Railways, or BR as the new organisation soon became known. The *Railway Magazine*, eager to prophecy what the new state livery would be, picked red as the obvious Labour

Right:
The LNER was already using Gill Sans lettering and numbers, so the transition to the interim style was easy. Class O4 2-8-0 No 63839 carries its new number at Cambridge in 1948.   *Colin Boocock*

Left:
In April 1948 the new BR renumbering scheme was announced and this publicity photograph was issued. The renumbering affected some 20,000 locomotives as they passed through the workshops for repairs. This numberplate, the first to carry a new BR five-figure number, was fixed to rebuilt 'Royal Scot' class 4-6-0 No 46124 *London Scottish*. It is seen in Crewe works whilst under repair on 12 April 1948. In fact the numberplate is not to BR style, using instead the former LMS style numerals. The BR style was plain Gill Sans as seen on the 8A shedplate below.
Ian Allan Library

Below:
Here is Bulleid 'West Country' class 4-6-2 No 34039 *Boscastle* newly painted in malachite green, posing at Stewart's Lane depot. The engine has the new BR numbering and lettering, all in SR style, and retains its SOUTHERN plate on the smokebox front. It was all soon to be very different!
Locomotive Publishing Co

Party choice and published an artist's impression of an LNER 'B1' 4-6-0 in pillar box red! In retrospect, perhaps it would have been a wiser choice than some which followed, although of course it had political implications that would have upset a great many people. There were also those who observed at the time that it did not really matter what colour they chose because it would soon disappear again under the dirt!

While the options on colours for locomotives and rolling stock were being considered, the former railways' liveries continued to appear for much of 1948. True, the old company designations LMS, LNER, GWR and SOUTHERN were painted over. Also, to avoid duplicating engine numbers for longer than necessary, numbers were given temporary prefixes, E for LNER types, M for LMS, S for SR and W for ex-GWR classes. The full wording, BRITISH RAILWAYS, was initially the preferred inscription for painting on tenders and side tanks, in the lettering styles of the old companies.

There was another problem to be overcome, about how to renumber the locomotives. Ideally, diesels

Below:
Whoever decided that the numberplate on the front of an 'A4' should be high up rather than just above the coupling had, in the Editor's view, little or no aesthetic sense! No 60028 *Walter K. Whigham*, in experimental dark blue lined in red, cream and grey, heads the 'Tees-Tyne Pullman', probably in 1949. It carries as yet no shedcode plate, its allocation being painted near the buffers, LNER style.
R. F. Dearden

and electrics should have been kept well clear of steam locomotive number ranges. Indeed an early proposal, illustrated by a touched-up photograph in the *Meccano Magazine*, showed a WR Prairie tank with a painted number like 66103! However, the WR gained someone's ear with its request to retain its cast numberplates, and so the numbers were revised to enable WR engines to keep their former GWR numbers. The final number ranges chosen were:

1- 9999	Western Region (former GWR) locomotives
10000-29999	Diesel and electric locomotives
30000-39999	Southern Region (former SR) locomotives
40000-59999	London Midland Region and Scottish Region (former LMS) locomotives

60000-69999	Eastern and North Eastern Regions and Scottish Region (former LNER) locomotives
70000-99999	Standard BR steam locomotives, and former WD austerity tender locomotives in BR ownership.

To give credit where credit is due, the Railway Executive, with R. A. Riddles in the chair for locomotives and rolling stock — termed as Member for Mechanical and Electrical Engineering — was

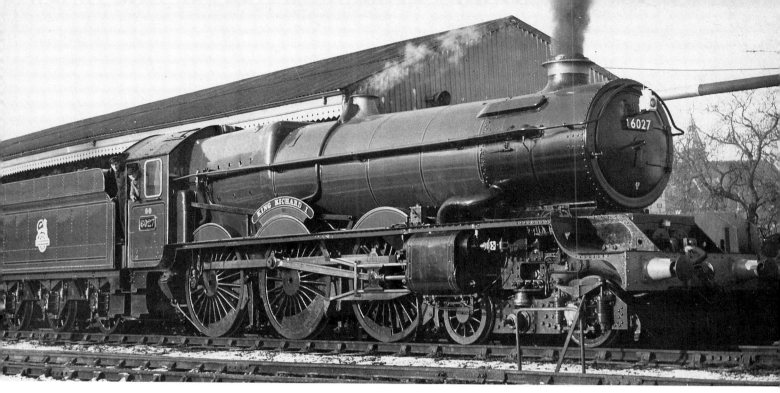

Above:
**Experience with the blue livery in everyday service
conditions soon revealed that it did not stand up well and
faded in time. It was extremely difficult to retouch damaged
portions without creating a patchwork effect. The Railway
Executive therefore abandoned the blue, and the
Brunswick green was substituted for all principal
passenger engines as they passed through the workshops.
Fresh from the Swindon paintshop, 'King' class 4-6-0
No 6027 *King Richard I* is seen on a running-in turn at Bath
Spa, around January 1955, in green livery.**   *K. H. Leech*

remarkably speedy in selecting new BR liveries.
This was without question to create public relations
in their favour, faced as they were by much hostility
and old company loyalty.

In January 1948 the Railway Executive was
treated to a small exhibition of locomotives (LMS
Class 5s) painted in the shades of green used by the
former companies. The locomotives were paraded
past eyes which were not altogether appreciative.

Following this, in May 1948 a series of named
trains on all Regions was presented with
locomotives and carriages decked out in
experimental colours. Class 7P locomotives to haul
them received deep ultramarine blue, Class 6P (a
'Castle', a rebuilt 'Jubilee' and a 'Lord Nelson' are
known to have been so treated) shone out in light
apple green, and the carriages bore deep plum lower
panels and off-white upper panels, reminiscent
again of the former London & North Western
Railway (LNWR) coaching stock colours. All the
locomotives were lined out in red, cream and grey.

The carriage colours soon gained the nickname
'plum and spilt milk'! The green locomotives looked

Left:
**This Hastings to Charing Cross train, photographed near
Tonbridge, is fully (almost) in the standard BR style. The
'Schools' class 4-4-0, No 30924 *Haileybury*, is in black, lined
red, cream and grey and the coaches are carmine and cream,
except for a green one at the rear.**
Eric Treacy/Millbrook House Collection

fine, except that the lining clashed aesthetically
with the base colour. In service the plum and spilt
milk did not prove to last well, the blue was thought
to be too dark, and the green was not popular either.

A good design feature introduced with the
experimental liveries was the use of Gill Sans
lettering and figures on all locomotives and rolling
stock. These letters displaced the former railways'
lettering styles for a short period when locomotives
were still being repainted in the old liveries, and
became standard later when the new, standard
colours were decided upon.

Standard Styles

As already observed, the public — or at least those
who showed some interest — did not react very
enthusiastically to the experimental liveries, but the
Railway Executive was not daunted, because it
knew that a decision had to be made. The new
standard colours that were adopted are described in
detail later in this book.

Suffice it to say here that a lighter shade of blue
was adopted for top link express engines, lined out
in black and white; other express locomotives
received Brunswick green, close to the GWR shade,
lined out in black and orange; mixed traffic and
lesser passenger engines retained the lined black
style using LNWR style lining; freight locomotives
were unlined plain black.

Brighter colours than ever seen before were to
adorn the carriage stock. Main line corridor
coaches became carmine red and cream, while
non-corridor stock was to be plain red, both groups
being lined out in black and gold.

The reader will note that I use the description
carmine red for the carriage stock, for this was
indeed the shade chosen. However, the official
publicity described it as crimson lake, which in all

truth it in no way resembled! An unofficial and unflattering description was coined by railway enthusiasts of the day, who called it 'blood and custard'. Perhaps it would have been more acceptable if the locomotives had been in carmine red as well. Only the lined black locomotives seemed to match the scheme to a certain extent.

Widespread use of the words BRITISH RAILWAYS on engines and tenders was only a first step, because the British Transport Commission (BTC) wanted each executive to have its own symbol or totem. Thus a new totem was required by the Railway Executive. The first offering was an elongated version of the famous London Transport totem. This was used on all stations as the base for the smaller station nameplates, and also appeared on road vehicles carrying the words BRITISH RAILWAYS. But the trial of a large one of these on the tender of a 'Schools' class 4-4-0 looked hideous.

The BTC also produced a totem for all its undertakings, the well known lion straddling a wheel, with, in BR's case BRITISH RAILWAYS in full across the wheel centre. While projecting quite a strong image, this was not strictly an heraldic device. It was designed by the graphic artist Abram Games. The lion faced forwards on locomotives, so left-facing and right-facing versions were required. Small and large size totems were provided, to suit the different dimensions of the fleet to which they were to be applied. Thus it was the BTC totem that was used on BR locomotives and multiple-units, while the official BR totem stayed on stations, lorries and on stationery and publicity material!

Gradually the new colours, totems and lettering began to make an impact, even if a slightly confusing one, and as the colour schemes were painted over, the memories of the Big Four began to fade a little, although there was continued loyalty.

Changes

It was not long before day-to-day wear and tear demonstrated that the blue chosen for the premier express passenger locomotives was unable to maintain a reasonable appearance, when compared with the green or black locomotives. As a result, the blue was quite soon officially abandoned, and the Brunswick green substituted. With today's paint technology such a decision would not have been necessary, but the quality of paint and methods of application then typical were governed by a need to keep costs low, and the pigment could not withstand rough treatment without revealing it. By contrast, both the green and the black could be 'patch-painted' (ie retouched) more easily, because they did not fade so badly.

This is an appropriate moment to pause and review the livery scene as it was in the early 1950s. After the abandonment of the blue there remained the Brunswick green, lined black and plain black liveries. The black locomotives looked smart when clean, but incredibly drab when neglected. The

Brunswick green looked fine on ex-GWR locomotives, where it was embellished by much brass and copper; it looked less happy on the majority of the other types, and positively dull when dirty. The red and cream carriages (and plain carmine) had a certain brightness but little charm. Standards of cleaning did begin to improve a little, but an atmosphere of steam and smoke still ruled the day.

Just when it seemed that, for better or worse, a standard, nationalised railway image and livery had been established, politics again intervened! This was due to the return to power of a Conservative government, pledged against nationalisation and intent upon reorganising the railways in Regional groups of workable size with increased autonomy. The idea was to re-create the old sense of rivalry and stimulate loyalties.

Under the Conservatives' 1953 Transport Act the Railway Executive was abolished and the BTC became directly responsible for each Region, appointing managers ('officers') with increased status and power. This abolition of the Railway Executive and the strengthening of Regional influence led to public speculation that the old railways' colours would soon be seen again on Britain's trains. The BTC however, preferred to hold to standardisation and retained firm control of such matters as traction and rolling stock design and manufacture. Nonetheless, few people were surprised when the announcement came that some Regional liveries were to be restored.

What was surprising was the piecemeal way it was done. As I later wrote in my book *British Rail 1948-83, A Journey by Design* (Ian Allan, 1983).

'First of all there was the predicted move towards Regional identities, a move which seemed to go astray before it had begun. "Slowly but surely the old Great Western is coming back to us," wrote the editor of *Trains Illustrated* in March 1956. "Now we hear that this summer the 'Cornish Riviera Express', 'Torbay' and 'Bristolian' expresses will be equipped with chocolate and cream-painted coaching stock — though oddly enough, it seems that the stock concerned will be BR standard, not ex-GW!" Well, it could have been worse. The Eastern Region could have got away with its scheme to reinstate its team of painters, stainers and grainers in order to paint imitation teak upon its Standard coaches of all-steel manufacture for the Great Eastern section.'

As it was, the decision did not have the expected results on the Southern Region. Certainly, green carriages were to emerge again from the carriage works at Lancing and Eastleigh. Strangely, many SR carriages still carried malachite green, having been repeatedly revarnished at overhauls rather than be painted red, or red and cream! The new green was somewhat darker and less garish than malachite (it is sold in modelling circles under the name of 'BR stock green', which term I shall use henceforth in this book). In contrast to the previous

SR rate of change, most coaches received new coats of plain, unlined green paint at their next overhauls, and the demise of red and cream on the SR was unexpectedly swift!

However, apart from the selected trains on the WR which were honoured with chocolate and cream livery, all other coaching stock on BR was repainted LMS maroon, lined out in standard BR style. Thus was removed, for ever, the last brightly coloured

Below:
'V2' 2-6-2 No 60803 in standard lined black livery pulls out of Lincoln Central southbound for King's Cross. The 'V2s' were among several other classes to receive green livery in later BR years. *R. E. Vincent*

Above:
Dirt was the main enemy of locomotive paintwork. This 'B16' 4-6-0 leaving York on a Birmingham train on 20 May 1953 has lost its gloss though its lining is still visible. The carriages are in carmine red and cream.
Eric Treacy/Millbrook House Collection

carriage livery of the steam age, as henceforth most of our passenger trains north of the Thames were to carry dull maroon livery until steam had nearly finished its lifespan.

The summer of 1956 saw the appearance of a new emblem to replace the emaciated lion-over-wheel. This, the BTC announced, comprised 'a demi-lion rampant (the British lion) holding between the paws

a silver locomotive wheel. The lion is issuant from a heraldic crown of gold on which are arranged the rose (for England), the thistle (for Scotland), the leek (for Wales) and the oak leaf (for all Great Britain)'. The legend BRITISH RAILWAYS was retained in rather weak lettering, and the lion still had a noticeable lack of anatomy. It was, at best, only a slight improvement upon the first version, and visually it was definitely out of keeping with the progress of modernisation that was by now gaining pace.

The same period also saw the reintroduction of a shade of crimson lake on the Stanier Pacifics of the London Midland Region (not the Scottish) to match the carriages. Apart from some initial experiments with standard orange and black lining, the red engines were lined, LMS style, with cream and black edging.

The Last Years

There were two phases wherein Regional decisions began to influence steam locomotive liveries on British Railways. In the late 1950s, in addition to the first step towards painting LMR Pacifics red, there was a positive move on the Southern and Western Regions to upgrade the colours on some smaller passenger or mixed-traffic classes. Thus the Maunsell 'Schools' class 4-4-0s, which had

previously been branded worthy only of lined black livery, emerged from Eastleigh Works painted Brunswick green.

On the WR the 'Halls', 'Granges' and 'Manors' were repainted green to good effect. More surprisingly so were some Prairie tanks and even a few of the little 14XX 0-4-2Ts which worked branch line push-pull trains!

The 1960s also saw the WR include BR Standard Class 5 and Class 4 4-6-0s in the lined green livery. Indeed later, for a while almost any locomotive that went through Swindon Works was repainted green. Lesser types were unlined, and these included small Prairie tanks, BR Class 4 4-6-0s and Class 3 2-6-2Ts, 43XX 2-6-0s and BR Class 2 2-6-0s.

Otherwise, one can only report on the decaying of styles towards the end of the steam era. Many engines had their lining omitted at repaints. Sadly, other casualties were the metal adornments such as nameplates and numberplates, which were taken off, or stolen, or just not replaced after works attention. Worse, ex-GWR 4-6-0s were sometimes to be seen without their cabside numberplates, and even their brass safety valve covers went missing.

Carriages, particularly plain maroon ones, were being outshopped from some works bereft of any trace of lining out. On the LMR in particular, the painting of lining on locomotives was also dropped in the mid-1960s to save time and money. Class 5s came out of Crewe in plain black, as did 2-6-4Ts, 2-6-2Ts and other classes which were formerly adorned. The nadir, in the Editor's opinion, was the emergence from Crewe of the last BR Standard Pacific to be overhauled, No 70013 *Oliver Cromwell*, which was painted plain Brunswick green. This engine which was to gain fame as one which hauled special excursions on the official 'last day of steam' in 1968.

The ultimate degradation — when all the colour disappears under the dirt! 'Britannia' 4-6-2 No 70011 *Hotspur* is mechanically sound as it roars away from Cambridge with an up Liverpool Street express of mixed BR and LNER design carriages. Note how the lining out of the coaches does not match between adjacent vehicles. *Colin Boocock*

1. THE 1948 HYBRID AND EXPERIMENTAL LIVERIES

As I have explained in the Introduction, the first visual manifestation of nationalisation was an instruction to the railway workshops to paint out the company initials — LNER, LMS, GWR and the name SOUTHERN — as locomotives passed through for repairs. New locomotives emerged with no identification of ownership on them. The words BRITISH RAILWAYS, in full, were to be applied instead, on locomotive tenders and tank sides. The earliest examples retained the varied lettering styles of the former Big Four companies. Hence the Southern used its 'sunshine' lettering style, the London Midland used a plain 'grotesque' sans serif, the Western Region used the former GWR block Egyptian shaded style and the Eastern used Gill

Sans. The various existing livery colours were continued until paint stocks ran out, and many locomotives received intermediate repairs in which their old colours were retouched and the words

Right:
The first attempts to label locomotives under nationalised ownership used the former railways' colours and lettering, with the running numbers prefixed to indicate the former owners. Thus this Class J69 0-6-0T sported LNER green, BRITISH RAILWAYS in the former LNER Gill Sans lettering, and an E prefix to the number 8619. The number was still carried on the buffer beam.
Colour-Rail/T. B. Owen

Below right:
Class 5 4-6-0 No M5101 demonstrates what, to the Editor, is a rather clumsy attempt to incorporate the interim numbering system of prefix letters on to its LMS-type smokebox door numberplate. It is passing Wortley on the former Great Central while working a Manchester London Road to Marylebone train during the 1948 locomotive exchanges. *Austin Brackenbury*

Below:
Apart from BRITISH RAILWAYS on the tender and the painted E over the stainless steel numbers on the cabside, *Mallard* is to all intents and purposes still in LNER livery in this 1948 photograph. *Ian Allan Library*

BRITISH RAILWAYS added. No transfers were available, so all these locomotives were lettered by hand — quite a lengthy business in the case of the Western Region and Southern Region examples.

Then came the edict that Gill Sans was to be standardised and that smokebox numberplates should be carried as in LMS practice (except that the former LNWR 0-8-0s never received numberplates, neither on the LMS nor on BR! Neither did the Isle of Wight engines carry smokebox numberplates). It was the first step towards a unified livery scheme, even though the old colours were still being applied.

To begin with, the Gill Sans was hand painted, then transfers were supplied and production of cast iron smokebox numberplates got under way. Two sizes of smokebox numbers were used, the WR using a slightly larger size (5in letter height) to enable the four-figure numbers to fill a numberplate of about the same size as other Regions' five-figure plates which had 4in-high numerals. (Yet the BR Standard types had 5in-high five-figure numbers!)

The Western Region posed a problem, as mentioned earlier, in that all its locomotives carried cast brass or iron cabside numberplates. Any scheme to renumber the BR fleet had to take these into account, on the grounds of the high cost if they were replaced (though it would have been less expensive had they been disposed of and the engine numbers painted on! — Editor). Hence the WR locomotives retained their original numbers and to begin with had a Regional prefix W painted above or below the plate on the cabside.

The other Regions began this temporary identification system, prior to the comprehensive renumbering scheme (already described in the Introduction). Some LMR locomotives carried smokebox numberplates with the M prefix added. On the SR this scheme led to even more complicated numbering on some Bulleid Pacifics when the prefix was added to their already complex system of recognition, eg s21C146!

When the fully comprehensive renumbering scheme came into force, in most cases the locomotives retained their existing numerical digits with (in the case of SR locomotives) 30000 added; for LMS engines the addition was 40000 and for LNER 60000. There were several exceptions to this pattern. Bulleid's Pacifics, and also his 'Q1' 0-6-0s, were given new number series between 33000 and 35030. Many older LMS engines that were previously numbered above 20000 had new numbers allotted to them in the 58000 series, and many other adjustments were made to other engines formerly in the 10000 series to fit them in. On the LNER, new construction of 'B1' 4-6-0s led to renumbering of some 'B16' 4-6-0s to make way for them, and on at least one occasion two engines were seen together with virtually the same number, the 'B16' with the E prefix, and the 'B1' with the five-figure number in place.

Above:
LNER apple green looked fine on locomotives of all sizes. This Scottish 'B12' 4-6-0 had received its new BR number, 61508, and BRITISH RAILWAYS on its tender, but was otherwise still in full LNER lined green livery when photographed at Kittybrewster in 1948.
Colour-Rail/J. M. Jarvis

Below:
Other Regions also started renumbering locomotives by using the lettering styles of the former railways. Adams 'Radial' 4-4-2T No 30584 carries former SR 'sunshine' lettering, and also has the new standard smokebox door number plate.
Colour-Rail/B. J. Swain

Left:
Because the words BRITISH RAILWAYS had to be painted by hand until suitable transfers became available, a very time-consuming operation, many locomotives left the works with blank tender or tank sides. In this condition is 'N15X' 4-6-0 No 32333 *Remembrance*, **still in SR malachite green, hauling freight past Bramshott Halt in November 1951. The wagons include several in former brown livery plus two in the BR light grey used for wagons not fitted with continuous brakes. Near the back of the train is a wagon with an unpainted board following repair, not an uncommon sight in those days. The white diagonal stripe on the third wagon denotes the position of the end door for tippling.**
Colour-Rail/T. B. Owen

Below:
The LNER bequeathed to BR the Grimsby & Immingham Tramway whose cars were in teak livery. Car No 6 was still lettered BRITISH RAILWAYS as late as 1956.
Colour-Rail/T. J. Edgington

These early essays in corporate colours and styles I choose to call the hybrid liveries. They gave rise to some interesting sights. For example, in Scotland the attractive 'B12' 4-6-0s of Great Eastern lineage were being painted by Inverurie works in LNER apple green and looked fine with BRITISH RAILWAYS in full on their tenders. Likewise, the SR had its Royal 'T9' 4-4-0 which it did not have the heart to paint black, and this also received full malachite green with sunshine lettering, and was still so adorned in the early 1950s! So also were a handful of 'M7' 0-4-4Ts which the SR kept in public view as Waterloo station pilots, though these had Gill Sans lettering and numbers on the tank and bunker sides. Ashford and Brighton works managed to repaint several 'L1' 4-4-0s and Marsh Atlantics in malachite green with full BR numbers and lettering before the standard colours were demanded of them. So also did the ER receive garter

blue 'A4s' and apple green 'A3s' and 'B1s' with their BR numbers and BRITISH RAILWAYS on their tenders.

Meanwhile the first experimental liveries were being formulated under the Railway Executive, at the request of the BTC. Old company loyalties and personal bias played some part in these, and it can be said in retrospect that no attempt was made to produce an entirely new BR colour scheme, which was indeed a mistake. Instead, various existing alternatives were displayed. This display was arranged as a private BTC exhibition at Kensington Addison Road station at the end of January 1948. Riddles gathered together all the interested parties on the station platform and had the display set up around three brand-new Stanier 'Black 5s', plus an SR electric locomotive and some carriages. The three 'Black 5s' were Nos M4762 painted in SR malachite green, M4763 painted in LNER apple

Left:
Fowler 'Patriot' 4-6-0 No 45515 Caernarvon has received its BRITISH RAILWAYS and its new number in Gill Sans style, but otherwise still carries postwar LMS black livery, lined in maroon and straw. This Euston to Holyhead train climbing Camden bank includes many coaches still with LMS lettering. *Eric Treacy/Millbrook House Collection*

Below left:
LNER garter blue 'A4' 4-6-2 No 60033 Seagull with its train of teak-painted Thompson stock working the up 'Capitals Limited' near Hadley Wood only has its numbering and tender lettering to denote BR ownership. *R. F. Dearden*

Above right:
Non-standard numerals and lettering appeared on locomotives frequently during the early months after nationalisation. Neither the smokebox door numberplate nor the painted (probably by hand) lettering fully complied with the intended Gill Sans standard, on Stanier 2-6-2T No 40149, seen near Elstree with a fast commuter train. *F. R. Hebron/Rail Archive Stephenson*

Centre right:
The first Peppercorn Class A1 4-6-2 was delivered new soon after nationalisation (being greeted by at least one newspaper as the first BR Standard engine!). No 60114, in LNER apple green but otherwise declaring its BR ownership, speeds along the East Coast main line in July 1948. *E. R. Wethersett*

Right:
The need to hand-paint so many letters and numbers caused a number of locomotives to escape from receiving the full BRITISH RAILWAYS on their tenders, which were left plain. In this picture, 'West Country' class 4-6-2 No 34035 Shaftesbury now has its correct smokebox door numberplate, but the engine and tender are still in malachite green. It was photographed near Worting Junction with a down milk train in April 1949. *M. W. Earley*

Above:
The experimental light apple green livery for secondary express passenger engines is seen here on rebuilt 'Patriot' 4-6-0 No 45531 *Sir Frederick Harrison* outside the paintshop at Derby in 1948. Note the cylinders are in green, and that the former LNWR red, cream and grey lining does not adequately offset the base green colour.
Colour-Rail/J. M. Jarvis

green and M4764 in GWR Brunswick green. Each locomotive was fully lined out, but only on the side nearest the platform, the other side being left plain! Riddles afterwards told me that no one could decide anything and that (as a private joke) he had secretly arranged for another Class 5 to pass the assembled managers, working a freight on the running lines. This, he had personally persuaded the Crewe paint shop to finish in full LNWR lined black livery. This really put the cat among the pigeons because everyone agreed that it looked very smart!

But the BTC was still insistent upon colour, so the next stage was to prepare repainted locomotives and carriages in time for the 1948 summer timetable workings. This second stage involved considerably more rolling stock and locomotives, because the idea was to have the proposed colours on display all over the BR system, in order to give the public a chance to see them and to comment. A fresh range of colours was selected, but all had their origins in the past, even if they were slightly modified. A curious omission was that the LMS crimson lake was not tried out on locomotives. It is said that this was because there was a very large LMS influence at Railway Executive headquarters, and it was felt that use of LMS red would be like rubbing salt into the wounds!

None of the liveries was, as already stated, entirely new, and some even dated back to pregrouping days, and to the LNWR in particular! This was undoubtedly because R. A. Riddles was himself a former LNWR man and had a decided preference for that company's livery of locomotives in lined black and carriages in 'plum and spilt milk'. Years later, over a splendid lunch at his London club, he told the author that his belief in black for locomotives was based on the proven grounds of economy and ease of retouching — a sound case indeed.

However, as I said already, the BTC wanted colours, and Riddles therefore had to abandon his preference. He ordered a range of alternative colours — deep ultramarine blue, and apple green, as well as lined black to be tried out. But in each case, true to his opinions, he had them lined out in the full LNWR style of red, cream and grey! The cream was a yellowish shade, and the Gill Sans lettering and numerals were matched with it.

The trials to gain public opinion were not received with much enthusiasm, and in the case of the bright green locomotive livery, and the plum and spilt milk carriages, day-to-day operating conditions soon showed them as unsuitable and difficult to

Above:

Class A4 4-6-2 No 60028 *Walter K. Whigham* carries the BR experimental dark blue with red, cream and grey lining; photographed at Grantham shed in August 1948.

Colour-Rail/J. M. Jarvis

Below:

A private exhibition of liveries was held for BTC and Railway Executive officers in Marylebone station early in 1948. Stanier 'Black 5' No 45292 was painted in experimental ex-LNWR lined black and is seen here attached to suburban stock in maroon livery. The locomotive's smokebox door numberplate is in former LMS style figures. In the left background, LMS main line stock displays the 'plum and spilt milk' colours. *Steam & Sail*

keep presentable. The dark blue locomotive livery (an almost purple shade on some ER Pacifics) just darkened down to become almost black, while, as always, the lined black locomotives looked smart if kept clean. A pale shade of blue was used on one SR electric locomotive, No CC2, with silver lining and lettering — it looked, to say the least, somewhat anaemic. The only positive early decision was to perpetuate Bulleid's SR malachite green for all EMU stock, which of course was another well established livery. The rest of the BR fleet was to be the subject of debate throughout 1948.

The summer 1948 experimental liveries can be summarised as follows:

Locomotives

Express Passenger Types:

Deep ultramarine blue for boiler, cab, cylinder covers and tender, lined red, cream and grey; vermilion red buffer beams; all othe parts black. Locomotives known to have carried these colours are LMR 'Princess Coronation' class 4-6-2s, ER 'A4' and 'A3' 4-6-2s and WR 'King' class 4-6-0s. On the SR a solitary 'Merchant Navy' class Pacific was tried briefly in a bizarre scheme of blue with broad red parallel lines.

Other Passenger Classes:

Bright apple green for boiler, cab and firebox and cylinder covers, and tender, lined red, cream and grey; vermilion red buffer beam, all other parts black. Locomotives known to have carried these colours are LMR 'Rebuilt Patriot' and 'Jubilee' 4-6-0s, ER 'Sandringham' 4-6-0s, SR 'Lord Nelson' 4-6-0s and WR 'Castle' class 4-6-0s.

Mixed Traffic Types:

A selection of locomotives on each Region appeared in LNWR style lined black at this time, although not specifically allocated to the carriage stock in the experimental liveries.

Freight Locomotives:

All freight and shunting locomotives were to be painted plain gloss black for boiler, cab, cylinder covers and tender. Buffer beams were vermilion red; all other parts base black.

Passenger Carriages (Locomotive Hauled)

Complete rakes of stock were repainted and kept together for specific services throughout the summer period. These featured the former LNWR livery of deep plum lower panels with off-white upper panels. The lining was old gold and black, with grey roofs and black undergear. The more important express services were chosen to put the colours well in the public eye.

Freight Stock

No particular effort seems to have been directed towards freight stock liveries at this early stage, and the Regions continued to paint in their usual shades of grey, bauxite red, or umber brown. Chocolate brown was used by the WR for some vans which also ran in passenger trains; likewise maroon by the LMR and green by the SR.

Below:
The hurry to put new locomotives into traffic in the late 1940s, as Britain's railways recovered from the effects of war, caused much painting work to be skimpy. New 'Merchant Navy' class 4-6-2 No 35026 was delivered by Eastleigh works in unlined malachite green, temporarily coupled to a tender which was also plain green but of a lighter shade and which was intended for a Brighton-built light Pacific. In the Editor's view this effect was not impressive. The train is an up Weymouth-Waterloo express climbing the 1 in 60 of Parkstone bank on 10 June 1949.
H. Weston

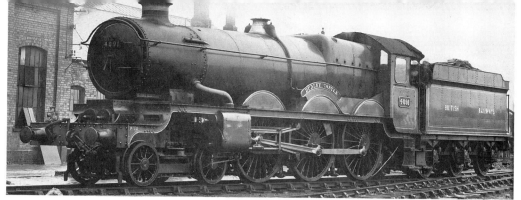

Left:
The experimental light green colour did not really suit a 'Castle' 4-6-0. No 4091 *Dudley Castle* had been fully painted in apple green with red, and grey lining. Western Region clearly did not relish using full size Gill Sans lettering for the BRITISH RAILWAYS on the tender! The numerals on the smokebox door numberplate are also smaller than standard.
W. J. Reynolds

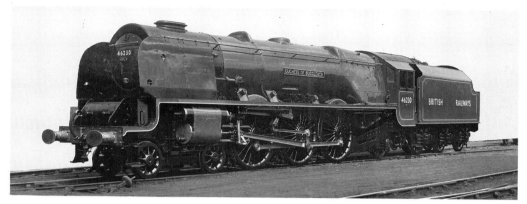

Left:
A posed photograph of newly painted 4-6-2 No 46230 *Duchess of Buccleuch* shows well the detail of the experimental blue livery for top link locomotives. Lined in red, cream and grey, the cabside numerals and the tenderside lettering are different sizes. The power code 7P appears below the running number. There are thin red lines on the cylinder and boiler lagging bands. The cylinders are blue. *Ian Allan Library*

Above left:
'Princess Royal' 4-6-2 No 46209 *Princess Beatrice* shows its red, cream and grey lining on the cabside as it ascends the grade at Shap Wells with a Birmingham to Glasgow train.
Eric Treacy/Millbrook House Collection

Left:
Caledonian 0-6-0 No 57621, seen near Carlisle, is in full unlined black interim livery, though minus its shed allocation plate.
Eric Treacy/Millbrook House Collection

27

2. THE 1949 BRITISH RAILWAYS STANDARD LIVERIES

Above:
The new standard colour finally chosen in 1949 for top link express engines was a version of Caledonian blue, which clearly suited the handsome form of Stanier Pacific No 46231 *Duchess of Atholl*. Lining was black and white. Cylinders and smoke deflectors were black.
Colour-Rail/W. H. Foster, Courtesy the L&YR Saddle-tank Fund

Left:
Controversy will always rage over whether blue suited the former Great Western 'King' class 4-6-0s. Readers can judge for themselves from this picture of No 6000 *King George V* photographed at Chippenham in July 1949.
Colour-Rail/K. H. Leech

The durable Brunswick green lasted until the end of steam and was for many people probably the best loved of the various liveries. BR standard Class 7 Pacific No 70037 *Hereward the Wake* (with nameplate backed in unofficial red) pulls away from London's Liverpool Street station with a morning express to Norwich. Main line stock is seen in carmine and cream livery and suburban coaches in plain carmine, and former LNER teak. *Steam & Sail*

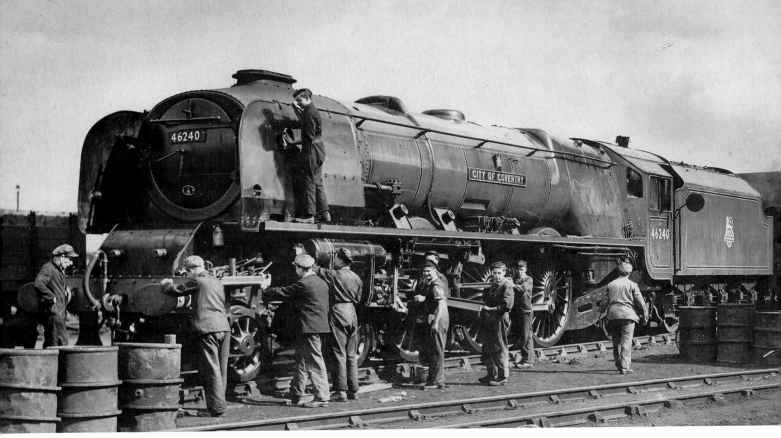

Above:
City of Coventry, No 46240, carries the full standard blue livery for top link expresses, with black and white lining and the large size BR totem. Even with the efforts of all these cleaners at Camden shed, the blue paintwork appears patchy. It was the unreliability of the blue pigment to maintain a consistent shade that led to the decision to eliminate this colour on BR.
F. R. Hebron/Rail Archive Stephenson

In the spring of 1949 the Railway Executive announced the details of its new range of standard liveries, to be adopted in future for locomotives, rolling stock, road vehicles and so forth.

The decisions were made! As to whether or not they were correct, or the best ones for the time, is a matter of debate. They were, in the author's opinion, a weird combination of colours and they did not add up to an attractive overall image. But before describing them, a further experiment should be mentioned, notably in connection with the 1948 blue locomotives.

This colour seems to have provoked the most reactions and the most problems. The first experiments had concentrated on a deep ultramarine blue (similar to the old Great Eastern Railway livery) although one ER class 'A3' locomotive carried what can only be described as purple due to a predominance of red pigment in the paint supplied. Someone evidently suggested trying a lighter shade of blue, and the old Caledonian Railway (CR) shade of blue was suggested as being suitable. Students of railway history will doubtless know that more than one shade of CR blue existed in Caledonian days — the colour being attained by hand mixing Prussian

blue and white. Some CR locomotives carried a very light shade, others a much darker version. Whoever supplied the BR paint sample chose the lightest shade, and in little time it betrayed every speck of dust and sign of wear. So the colour was modified to a more medium shade — using Bulleid 'Merchant Navy' Pacific No 35024 as the guinea pig. (This locomotive underwent three repaints in different shades of blue inside one year!)

Likewise the bright apple green of the experimental locomotives had aroused some dislike, being considered too sickly, and before the final schemes were announced at least one ER 'Sandringham' 4-6-0 was repainted in authentic LNER apple green (a shade or two darker than the BR one, and with a touch more blue in it), but with LNWR style lining. It was to no avail however and Brunswick green was substituted, complete with GWR style black and orange lining, the only Big Four livery to be adopted by British Railways on its steam locomotive fleet.

Herewith are the details as announced by the Railway Executive in 1949. I would only remind the reader that where I have put 'carmine red', the Railway Executive quoted 'crimson lake', and where I show 'gold' one should think in terms of an 'old gold' shade — a mix of yellow ochre and white — true gold leaf was not available!

Right:
Brunswick green soon replaced blue on the main line express engines, though many regretted that the A4s had to follow suit. Green 'A4' 4-6-2 No 60007 Sir Nigel Gresley takes the up 'Flying Scotsman' out of Newcastle Central. Its train is by now made up largely of new BR Mk 1 vehicles in carmine and cream livery. *Eric Treacy/Millbrook House Collection*

The 1949 Colour Schemes

Locomotives

1: Top Link Express Passenger Classes
Medium blue, lined black and white, on boiler, cabsides, side valances (except on ex-GWR) and tender; cab fronts and tender backs plain blue. Cylinder covers black lined white; smoke deflectors and side valances (ex-GWR only) plain black; buffer beams vermilion red. Nameplates and cabside numberplates backed in black (red on Southern Region). All other parts base black.
Types:

LMR Class 7P (later 8P) Pacifics
ER and NER Classes A1, A3, A4 and W1
WR 'King' class 4-6-0s
SR 'Merchant Navy' class Pacifics
ScR Class 7P (later 8P) Pacifics (ex-LMS) and classes 'A3', 'A4' and 'A10' (ex-LNER)

2: Other Express Passenger Types
Brunswick green, lined black and orange, on boiler, cabsides and tender sides; side valances (WR only), cab fronts and tender backs plain green; side valances (other than WR) green edged orange and black; cylinder covers black, lined orange; smoke deflectors plain black; buffer beams vermilion red. Nameplates and cabside numberplates backed in black. All other parts base black.
Types:

LMR Class 6P (later 7P) 'Royal Scot', rebuilt 'Patriot' and 'Jubilee'; Class 5XP (later 6P) 'Patriot' and 'Jubilee'
ER and NER Classes A2, B2, B3 and B17
WR 'Castle' and 'Star' class 4-6-0s
Southern Region 'West Country', 'Battle of Britain', 'Lord Nelson' and 'King Arthur' classes
ScR 'Royal Scot', 'Jubilee' and 'A2' classes

3: Lesser Passenger Types, and Mixed Traffic Classes
Black lined red, cream and grey on cab sides, tender sides and side valances (except that side valances on WR were plain black, unlined); boiler and cylinder covers black, lined red; buffer beams vermilion red. Nameplates and cabside numberplates backed in red. All other parts plain black.

4: Freight and Shunting Locomotives
Unlined gloss black; buffer beams vermilion red.

Above:
No 72006 *Clan MacKenzie*, one of the 10 BR Class 6 4-6-2s, poses outside Crewe works. Note the nameplate in official black, large size totem on the tender and unlined (incorrect) cylinder covers.
Colour-Rail/E. S. Russell

Below:
'West Country' class 4-6-2 No 34002 *Salisbury* poses at Eastleigh shed. The air-smoothed Bulleid Pacifics were lined out with two longitudinal black lines edged in orange. *Colin Boocock*

Rebuilt 'Merchant Navy' 4-6-2 No 35018 *British India Line*, seen at Southampton Central in 1956, is painted in the full, correct style for express engines. Note the single orange lining on the side valances, the double orange lines on the cylinder covers, black backed nameplate and power code (8P) above the running number on the cabside. The carmine paint on the coach behind No 35018's tender is becoming faded. Note the Southern Region carriage set number painted on the vehicle end. *Steam & Sail*

I have already commented upon the change in shade of blue which took place at the beginning of the programme. The finished shade was usually described as Caledonian blue. Because of the instability of its pigments the colour was not a satisfactory one with which to deck steam locomotives in a regime in which repainting was restricted to general overhauls every five years. The colour was not capable of retaining its shade long enough to be effectively retouched at intermediate overhauls and revarnished, as could the green and black locomotives.

All the classes listed in the first group were therefore subsequently repainted or painted in the Brunswick green livery as described in group 2. Early examples in the dark green livery had a deeper and richer shade than was subsequently standardised.

All locomotives were to carry the new lion-over-wheel totem on the tender or tanksides, and there were large or small versions in transfer form. All lettering and numerals were to be in Gill Sans, in light cream edged in black. Smokebox numberplates of cast iron also had numerals in Gill Sans; these were raised and painted white on a black background. The lower part of the smokebox was to carry a cast iron shedcode plate in former LMS style but in Gill Sans, again white on black; builder's worksplates and tender capacity plates were to be similarly treated unless finished in polished brass.

Passenger Carriages

5: *Main Line Corridor Stock and Full Brakes for Principal Trains*
Bodysides carmine red, with cream upper panels, lined gold and black. Vehicle ends, underframes and bogies, plain black. Roofs light grey.
6: *Non-corridor Coaches and Other Passenger Train Vans*
Bodysides carmine red, lined* gold and black. Vehicle ends, underframes and bogies, plain black. Roofs light grey.
*Many were not lined out in practice.

Freight Stock

7: *Wagons*

Unfitted —	Battleship grey
Fitted, Piped —	Orange brown
Insulated —	Stone (to be changed to white when paint became available)

All wagons were to be lettered and marked in white Gill Sans medium type, except on insulated stock which had black letters. All underframes and undergear to be plain black.

There were the original schemes. In due course the grey was of a lighter shade and the orange brown became bauxite red. The shortage of white paint is an interesting reflection on the continuing austerity of the postwar period!

Below:
On the other hand, former GWR locomotives, with their copper and brasswork shining, did look good in Brunswick green. BR built 4-6-0 No 7018 *Drysllwyn Castle* heads an express near Twyford. The mixture of BR and ex-GWR stock has the livery lines at different heights above the rail. This is due to the painting diagram tying the cream area to 1in above and below the windows, irrespective of their dimensions. Thus trains of mixed stock presented an untidy appearance as seen here in the middle of the train.
T. E. Williams

8: Containers

Orange brown, except insulated containers which were stone colour until white paint became available.

Once again, bauxite red later replaced the orange brown. Lettering was in white Gill Sans, or black on white painted containers.

NB For the benefit of modellers in particular, Appendix 1 gives more details of these liveries, adapted from contemporary official sources.

Above:
BR green 'A3' 4-6-2 No 60055 *Woolwinder* pulls out of King's Cross with a train for Leeds and Bradford. In common with most ex-LNER engines on the Eastern and North Eastern Regions, *Woolwinder* carries no power code over the running number, but does display the route availability (RA) number low on the cabside.
Eric Treacy/Millbrook House Collection

Below:
'Royal Scot' 4-6-0 No 46105 *Cameron Highlander* halts briefly at Tebay with the 4.20pm (Sundays) from Carlisle to Preston. The locomotive demonstrates correctly the complete Brunswick green livery with black and orange lining. *J. E. Wilkinson*

Facing page, top:
A full train in the standard livery for suburban workings comprises Class V3 2-6-2T No 67620 in lined black hauling coaches in plain carmine red. The carriage ends are painted black (note the articulated twin at the front of the train!); the locomotive carries no power class above its number but the former LNER route availability code, also used formally on BR, is seen on the tankside just above the cab steps. The Darlington station sign is in North Eastern Region tangerine with white lettering. The train is starting a trip to Richmond in May 1956.
Colour-Rail/J. Davenport

Facing page, bottom:
There is no doubt that gloss black, lined in red, cream and grey, was a superlative livery for steam locomotives when clean. Spotless, ex-works Class E1R 0-6-2T No 32697 stands in the snow at Eastleigh in January 1954. *Colour-Rail/T. B. Owen*

Above left:
The brightness of the standard carmine and cream livery of main line coaching stock shines out in this view of green 'King' class 4-6-0 No 6009 *King Charles II* as it leaves Dawlish with the 1.25pm from Paddington to Kingswear in July 1957. The 'double red' route availability discs can be seen on the cabside above the numberplate.
Colour-Rail/P. W. Gray

Left:
Facing the mountains of the Scottish Highlands is a Standard Class 5 piloting ex-LNER 'K2' 2-6-0 No 61789 *Loch Laidon* at Crianlarich on a Glasgow-Fort William train. The large size totem on the 'K2's tender may appeal to some readers.
Colour-Rail/G. W. Parry Collection

Right:

No two works ever seemed to interpret the painting instructions in the same way. This former Caledonian Railway 4-4-0 seen at Perth in BR lined black livery had no lining on the coupling rod splashers, a small size totem on the tender and large size numerals on the cab.

John Adams

Centre right:

The Western Region did not paint lining on the side valances of ex-GWR locomotives. It also did not display the BR power classification, preferring to retain the GWR disc and letter notation above the numberplate (the numberplate itself was an aberration in an otherwise standard set of styles). Many of the black engines also received non-standard red painted backgrounds to their nameplates (and cabside numberplates) as seen here on 'Hall' class 4-6-0 No 5985 *Mostyn Hall*. Nonetheless, the overall effect is excellent!

P. M. Alexander

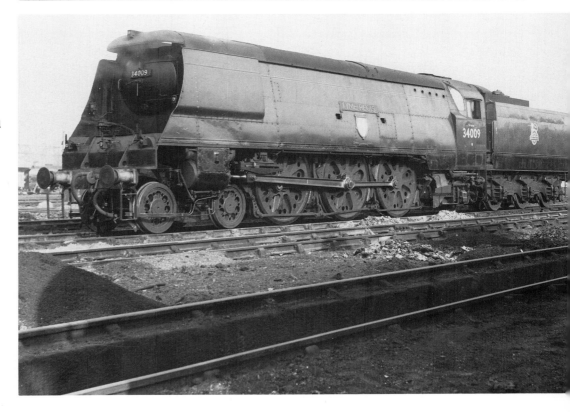

Below right:

A variation of the standard Brunswick green livery was essential for the air-smoothed Bulleid Pacifics. The black longitudinal lining bands were wider than standard and were edged in orange. (Please see Appendix 1 for details.) The small yellow disc painted below the running number on the cabside indicated the use of briquette water treatment. This disc was later changed to a triangle. The roof of the air-smoothed casing was black. No 34009 *Lyme Regis* was photographed at Nine Elms on 4 April 1959.

Colin Boocock

Left:
Plain black livery on a former Taff Vale Railway 0-6-2T is relieved slightly by the brass builder's plate on the front splasher. The smokebox door numberplate has only three numerals (5in height) but the plate is the standard length! No 351 was seen at Abercynon in June 1955.
Colour-Rail/T. B. Owen

Right:
A fine Midland Compound 4-4-0 speeds towards the fells demonstrating BR lined livery. The former LMS carriages on the train show how the practice of aligning the livery lines of the carmine and cream colours against the main window dimensions led to different heights on different coach designs. The LMS coaches had a wider red band above the windows than did other railways' stock. *Colour-Rail*

Below:
Plain black livery on Bulleid 'Q1' 0-6-0 No 33028 is unrelieved other than by the locomotive number, the tender totem, and the vermilion red buffer beam. The locomotive is seen at Ramsgate in October 1952.
Colour-Rail/T. B. Owen

Above:
Plain black livery was all that anyone expected to see on small tank engines. Adams Class B4 0-4-0 dock tank No 30089 rests at Eastleigh on 2 December 1958.
Colin Boocock

Below:
Goods engines were also all plain black, apart from the regulation red buffer beams. Former LSWR Class 700 0-6-0 No 30693 was at Eastleigh shed on 23 March 1959.
Colin Boocock

Above:
Coaching stock that was non-corridor and generally used for secondary or suburban duties was normally painted plain carmine red. Being a bright colour this did not make them unattractive. On the Southern Region at Gosport, this former LSWR push-pull set is smartly turned out in red, with the SR's set number (6) on the end. Most Southern Region coaches were operated in fixed set formations, sometimes without intermediate side buffers, and set numbers were rigidly applied.
Colin Boocock

Above left:
The livery for normal freight vehicles fitted with the vacuum brake was brown with white lettering, as seen on this new 13-ton open wagon. *BR*

Left:
Standing out among the relatively dull colours chosen for wagon stock was the use of white for insulated vehicles. This ex-LNER 12-ton fish van demonstrates white livery with black lettering. *BR*

3. THE 1956 REVISIONS

I have previously explained how the changed political scene in Britain in the mid-1950s influenced railway policy, and this change was to some extent reflected in BR liveries. Basically the same colours were retained for locomotives, but it is worthwhile to list the 1956 revisions (as they may be conveniently termed). Coincidental to these changes was the adoption of the revised lion-and-wheel totem. Gill Sans lettering was retained except for diesel shunting locomotives and a few small steam locomotives which, later on, received a condensed form of sans serif.

Below:
Maroon coaching stock illustrates one of the 1956 livery revisions. The Class 5 4-6-0 looks superb in the familiar, standard lined black colours, now set off by the 1956 totem on the tender side. This shot of No 45439 was taken as it passed Bushey on an up express in 1959. *Steam & Sail*

Locomotives

The most significant change at this time was the decision taken by the London Midland Region to paint its express passenger Pacifics in crimson lake. This applied to the Class 8P 'Princess Royal' and 'Duchess' classes only and excluded the Scottish Region-based examples which remained green. The BR Standard 'Britannias' allocated to the LMR also remained in lined green. A few of the crimson lake '8Ps' received BR style black and orange lining though without lining on the boiler lagging bands and with only a thin orange line along the bottom edge of the side valances; but the former LMS style of lining soon found favour and all the engines finally received this, with yellow lining edged with black. Cylinder covers were, by then uniquely among BR engines, not painted black but were in lined crimson lake. Buffer beams were in bright vermilion red, edged in yellow and black. (At about

Above:
Class 7P 4-6-0 No 46100 *Royal Scot* poses at Aston shed in classic Brunswick green livery. The electrification flashes date the photograph to post-1959 and it was in fact photographed in October 1961.   *Colour-Rail/T. B. Owen*

Below:
The crest on the tender is the only concession to the 1956 revisions to be seen on 'Jubilee' 4-6-0 No 45650 *Blake* at Nottingham Midland shed in September 1959.
Colour-Rail/Don Beecroft

this time the official BR colour for buffer beams was changed to signal red, a darker and less orange shade, but this did not apply to the LMR Pacifics.)

The new totem with the lion standing on a crown and holding a railway wheel in its paws appeared in two key versions and in several sizes. For locomotives the standard form was the one with the words BRITISH RAILWAYS extended either side of the central circle, rather on the lines of the Bulleid 'Merchant Navy' nameplates (though aesthetically it was far less satisfactory than these). There were two main sizes of this symbol to accord with the area available for it on different designs of locomotives and tenders. At the beginning the lion faced forwards when applied to either side of the locomotive or tender. Later it was decreed that, as the lion was taken directly from the BTC's heraldic crest, it always had to face the same direction as on the crest. As a result, from around 1957 the lion always faced left, irrespective of the side upon which it was used.

Passenger Carriages

As already described, three distinct liveries replaced the carmine and cream colours on express passenger stock. For principal trains on the WR a return to GWR chocolate and cream took place, lined in gold, yellow and black. For all Southern

Region services the new stock green was adopted with no lining out. For all other main line corridor coaches, irrespective of Region (Southern Region excepted) the standard livery became maroon with yellow and black lining. Carriage roofs were mid-grey, and underframes, carriage ends, bogies, etc were black. Lettering remained in Gill Sans style.

Non-corridor carriages (again except on the Southern Region where unlined stock green was used) were also changed to maroon, with the same lining. Some did actually escape without lining, but this was discouraged, except on non-passenger stock.

The use of stock green on Southern Region carriages did not match the Brunswick green of many of the locomotives which hauled them, a colour clash which to the Editor can only be regarded as inexcusable.

For the first time, the BR totem was applied to locomotive-hauled carriages. This version enclosed the lion-and-wheel inside a circular band displaying the words BRITISH RAILWAYS. Its appearance was

Below:
The revision of liveries in 1956 included the use of a totem based on the BTC's new heraldic crest. Most main line and suburban coaches were repainted lined maroon. This clean Class 5, No 45247, hauls a train of ex-LMS and BR Standard stock all in maroon livery past Wreay North in September 1962. *Peter J. Robinson*

Above:
No 45675 *Hardy*, standing at Willesden shed on 25 September 1960, seems well suited by its standard green paint, and displays the new BR standard totem on its tender. *Colin Boocock*

Left:
When the Bulleid Pacifics received tenders with cut-down side raves their cabsides were lined out to match. Thus they carried lining with the black line edged with orange on the air-smoothed casing, and with the orange lines separate from the black on the cab and tendersides. No 34106 *Lydford* waits for departure from St David's with the 5.21am from Exeter Central to Ilfracombe on 1 April 1964.

47

much more satisfactory than the locomotive version. The carriage totem was only applied to coaches intended for use on named trains. (It was also used on the motor coaches of multiple-units, in place of the older lion-over-wheel totem.)

One can recall only five instances of the carriage totem being applied to locomotive classes, two on the Southern, two on the Western and one on the Scottish, all on non-steam traction.

Freight Stock

Few significant changes were made to freight stock liveries at this stage of BR affairs. White had been introduced for fish vans and insulated containers, and the general rule was bauxite red for brake-fitted vehicles and mid-grey for unfitted. The only notable addition was on the shocvans introduced in this period which had their bodies on slides on the underframes, to cushion shunting shocks. These wagons were picked out with three broad white lines painted vertically on each side from the bottom upwards to about half-way up the bodyside. Also around this time the colour for demountable box containers was changed to maroon, with cream lettering.

Thus it can be said that, with the early demise of the blue colour for express engines, and the replacement of the bright red and cream coaching stock colours with relatively dull maroon, liveries on British Railways entered an uninteresting phase. Uniformity was attained, except on the Southern Region and on WR expresses, and except where loose carriages of the wrong colours got mixed! The colours that remained, Brunswick green, black, maroon, even Southern Region green, did not shine out in the modern world. Come 1965, the need for a new image had been acknowledged and (except on steam locomotives) all was thereafter to change.

Left:
At Plymouth Friary, ex-LSWR 0-4-4T No 30225 carries faded lined black with the 1956 totem.
Colin Boocock

Below:
Scotland did paint power codes on their former LNER locomotives, and also placed some of their smokebox door numberplates higher up than standard. 'B1' 4-6-0 No 61103 climbs Glenfarg bank with a freight train in which the grey painted wagons indicate the absence of continuous brakes.
Colour-Rail/J. G. Wallace

The most striking colour change in 1956 was the use of a shade of crimson lake on the LM Region's Stanier Pacifics. No 46245 *City of London* closely matches the maroon carriages of a Euston express at Birmingham New Street on 5 August 1963. The boiler plates are unlined, and the cab and tender are edged in black and cream.   *D. Mann*

Above:

Someone soon pointed out that the new totem, being an extract from a left-facing heraldic device, could not be reproduced facing right! On the tender of 'A4' 4-6-2 No 60017 *Silver Fox*, photographed at York, the lion in the totem faces the rear (correct).
Eric Treacy/Millbrook House Collection

Right:

On 6 May 1959 rebuilt 'West Country' 4-6-2 No 34010 *Sidmouth* was being prepared at Eastleigh shed. By the time this photograph was taken, Eastleigh works had adopted the practice of painting nameplates red.
Colin Boocock

Right:

No 46210 *Lady Patricia* takes water at Beattock station. The engine is in standard green livery while the ex-CR 0-4-4T shunting in the near background is lined black. *Lady Patricia's* totem on the tender side (incorrectly) faces right.
Eric Treacy/Millbrook House Collection

Above:
Green 'Princess Royal' 4-6-2 No 46203 *Princess Margaret Rose* **hammers up Beattock bank in August 1962 with a train of BR standard stock all in maroon. The Scottish Region maintained green livery for its Stanier Pacifics to the end.** *Peter J. Robinson*

Left:
GWR loyalties simply refused to die under nationalisation, and no one was very surprised when — given the opportunity in 1956 — the old chocolate and cream livery was restored for the carriages of some of the principal express trains, albeit with BR Mk 1 stock. The up 'Mayflower' is seen in Sonning cutting, hauled by 'King' class 4-6-0 No 6021 *King Richard III.*
M. W. Earley

Left:
Swindon began painting most of the locomotives which passed through the works Brunswick green. The 'Hall' class were given lined green livery, shown here on No 5901 *Hazel Hall,* **running near Mortimer with a Reading to Portsmouth train formed of SR coaches in stock green. The two greens clashed visually whenever they came together.** *M. J. Esau*

Great Western fans were delighted when the Western Region introduced brown and cream coaches again! No 6860 *Aberporth Grange*, at Penzance in August 1959, stands at the head of the up 'Royal Duchy' and carries the new WR style of train headboard. *Colour-Rail/G. J. Jefferson*

'Battle of Britain' 4-6-2 No 34054 *Lord Beaverbrook* hauls a short train of BR standard stock painted in the Southern Region's new stock green which was darker than the malachite green used by the former Southern Railway. Neither the carriage green nor the blue nameplate background are satisfactory aesthetically against the Brunswick green of the locomotive. The scene is at Raynes Park in June 1961. *Colour-Rail/J. P. Mullett*

Left:
The new totem looked satisfactory on the tanksides of modern 2-6-4Ts such as Stanier's three-cylinder machine No 42532, photographed at Cricklewood. *Colin Boocock*

Centre left:
Likewise, a BR Standard 2-6-4T looked smart in lined black. No 80035, seen at Willesden, even had its builder's plate neatly picked out with white lettering. *Colin Boocock*

Bottom left:
Even out in the Scottish Highlands the standard colours reigned supreme. Lined black 0-4-4T No 55263 brings a branch train up from Killin to Killin Junction in May 1960. The carriage is in plain maroon, not lined out. Note the inadequate application of the numeral transfers to the bunkerside — they run 'downhill'! *W. J. V. Anderson*

Top right:
Ashford works preferred to use the larger size of cabside numerals where it could. The line of the splashers on the ex-SECR 'L' class rendered this difficult. No 31777 was photographed at Bournemouth on the through train to Brighton on 21 March 1958, and its tender totem lion faces the wrong way. *Colin Boocock*

Centre right:
This Pickersgill 4-4-0 has the large version of the totem on its tender, which suits it well. No 54486 takes a southbound local goods south of Dunkeld in June 1959. *W. J. V. Anderson*

Right:
A Standard locomotive with standard lined black livery; Class 4 4-6-0 No 75026 rests at Eastleigh shed. *Colin Boocock*

Left:

The new crimson lake style looked magnificent on the 'Princess Coronation' 4-6-2s. No 46245 *City of London* was photographed on special duty at King's Cross station. Note the lining out of the tender frames, the red-painted cylinder covers, and the positions of the electrification flashes. The nameplates of the red engines were painted black. *Colour-Rail*

Right:

The 1956 carriage crest is seen at Mallaig in 1960 on the rear of the rebuilt ex-LNER 'beaver-tail' observation car. The vehicle is painted maroon and fully lined out in black and gold. The lettering OBSERVATION CAR on the coach sides is in 6in Gill Sans cream capitals. *Colin Boocock*

Below:

The first BR green used on the Grimsby & Immingham tramcars was a version of malachite, though the latest repaints may well have been done in stock green. Car No 26, a former Gateshead tram, was still active at Immingham on 18 October 1960. *Colin Boocock*

Right:
Other Regions might well have painted the running number of this 'Q' class 0-6-0 with larger numerals. No 30531 was in this condition when photographed on 23 March 1959. *Colin Boocock*

Below right:
BR standard suburban non-corridor coach No W43169 is in maroon livery lined out in black and old gold. The coach on the left is in unlined maroon. The one on the right (a former GWR vehicle) is in plain carmine red from the previous livery era. There were many years of running trains in mixed liveries — it is not just a modern trait!
Ian Allan Library

Right:
The BR lined black livery must have been good because it suited virtually every locomotive which received it. Adams 'O2' class 0-4-4T No 30199 is no exception. *Colin Boocock*

Right:
The North Eastern Region at Darlington works adopted a different style for black tank engines than did the other Regions. Class J72 0-6-0T No 68677, for example, though in standard plain black livery, had its running number below the totem on the tankside when it was seen at York station on 1 August 1959. *Colin Boocock*

58

4. VARIATIONS

I have already described in the Introduction the unofficial spread of Brunswick green among locomotive classes not officially authorised to carry it, including the use of unlined green on the WR and LMR. The economy of omitting lining out was a real saving in labour, the operation being quite time-consuming.

It is interesting that the standardised liveries on steam locomotives were observed to an extent in the

Below:
When 'Battle of Britain' class 4-6-2 No 34090 was named *Sir Eustace Missenden — Southern Railway* it was given a special livery of malachite green with not only the body stripes in yellow but the wheel tyre faces painted yellow as well! The engine carried the BR totem on the tender, and is seen here passing Folkestone Junction. *Rev A. C. Cawston*

breach by several of the workshops, which managed to interpret official instructions differently! Cowlairs in Glasgow, for example, used the large size cabside numerals on as many locomotives as they would fit, including the BR Standard 2-6-4Ts, even though officialdom dictated the smaller size. The lining out on the lined black engines was not always to the same thicknesses, either, as the observant reader browsing through the pictures in this book will note.

Ashford and Eastleigh works had different approaches to cabside lining. Eastleigh took the instruction literally that lining had to follow inside the cab edges by a fixed distance. In Ashford's view, to do that would cramp the lining where the cab side sheets were shortened by the curve down from the

Above:
No 73051 was one of three BR Class 5 4-6-0s originally delivered new to the Somerset & Dorset line in 1952. Later, the S&D depot at Bath Green Park was transferred from the Southern to the Western Region and No 73051 became part of WR stock, in time to be treated to a coat of lined green livery at a general overhaul when the fashion was to paint green almost anything that moved! *Steam & Sail*

Below:
In contrast, the late 1960s saw the LM Region in particular adopt simpler painting techniques abandoning the use of lining out. No 73069, seen at Stalybridge on 20 April 1968, looked sad in plain black. *Des Sheppard*

Below:
The use of Stroudley yellow on the Brighton works shunting locomotive had been a Southern Railway tradition for many years. No 377s, which became No DS377 under the British Railways numbering scheme for departmental engines, retained this striking style right to the end of its days. *Colour-Rail/J. M. Jarvis*

Above:
Departmental locomotives were generally plain black. Their ownership was usually added in small Gill Sans or script lettering on the side, the former style being illustrated in this view of Sentinel 0-4-0T No 40 (should it not have been DE40?) of the Eastern Region Civil Engineer's Department. This Class Y3 was photographed at Lowestoft sleeper depot in May 1953. *Colour-Rail/T. B. Owen*

running plate. Ashford works painted the lining as if the lower cabside was full width, running it off at the lower front edges — a somewhat neater effect.

On the Bulleid Pacifics, the air-smoothed casing did not lend itself to the normal standard lining method, and a compromise was reached. Instead of three solid yellow lines as was used when they were painted malachite green by the Southern Railway, BR agreed to two lining lines being painted the length of each side of the locomotive. The lines were black, edged in orange (or white on the blue engines), without the spacing between the black and orange (white) lines used on other locomotives.

The Western Region, always somewhat independent of thought, did not display the BR standard power classifications on former GWR-design locomotives. Thus, although the Western engines were given power codes by BR, Swindon applied the former GWR power code letters superimposed within that Region's route availability colour discs over the cabside numberplates. On other Regions' engines, small numerals and letters were painted over the locomotive number to indicate the power class. For a time in the 1950s, when the power codes were made more specific, depots would paint out the former code (say, 7) and use crude stencils and white paint for the new code. The Southern Region went into a phase of stencilling 7P 5FA on the cabsides of its 'West Country' class locomotives, for example. The codes were properly painted when the locomotives went through works subsequently. For some reason the BR power codes were not painted on former LNER locomotives except sometimes in Scotland.

The old LNER route availability code system was adopted by BR as standard (RA1 to RA9). The ER, NER, and sometimes the ScR, continued to apply them to the lower cabside panels in small letters and figures whereas the other Regions left them off. The Western Region continued its use of coloured discs, painted above the cabside numberplates.

Other cabside symbols were painted at different times. On the Southern Region, where water treatment using chemical briquettes was practised, locomotives which were fitted with the briquette holders in their tendertanks or sidetanks had a small yellow disc painted below the running number on the cabside. The habit of the SR engines of wandering on to the Western Region presumably caused confusion with the WR's route availability discs, because on the SR engines the disc was later replaced by a yellow triangle painted in the same position.

One sometimes saw a cream-coloured, five-pointed star painted on the cabside of a former LMS '8F' 2-8-0, below the running number. This denoted that the engine was one of those which had wheels balanced for 60mph running.

Early in 1949 there was one remarkable livery variation which occurred on the SR. On 15 February, 'Battle of Britain' 4-6-2 No 34090 was officially named *Sir Eustace Missenden*, as a tribute to Sir Eustace who was the railway's General Manager throughout World War 2. It was also intended as a tribute to the 67,000 SR employees who had worked through the dangerous and difficult war years, and in particular during the Battle of Britain (after which the class was named) when the SR was heavily attacked by enemy aircraft. For this prestigious event, No 34090 was painted in a special livery of malachite green, lined out in yellow, and with black trim. The new BR lion-over-wheel totem was carried on the tender sides, and the former Southern Railway coat of arms was featured on an enamel plaque on the locomotive itself, located between the two nameplates on each side of the air-smoothed casing. An unusual touch was the painting of the bogie and coupled wheels in malachite green with yellow tyre faces instead of black. In appearance the locomotive was somewhat smarter than the BR standard Brunswick green livery!

Mention must be made of an extraordinary adaptation of the standard carmine and cream livery. This was the idea of O. V. S. Bulleid, then Chief Mechanical Engineer of the Southern Region and who was known for his fertile imagination! This was the tavern car design which he had started to develop for the Southern Railway prior to 1948. The idea was to incorporate inside one end of a railway buffet car the ambience of a country public house, complete with beamed ceiling and bar stools! Outside, the red lower panels (only at the 'pub' end of the vehicle!) were lined out in a brickwork pattern, above which, on the cream panels, were painted replica wall beams and an inn sign. The cars were not a complete success and were soon rebuilt in more conventional form, and the ludicrous brickwork painted out.

Enthusiasts were pleased when the Eastern Region adopted a policy of painting station pilot locomotives in the colours of the pregrouping railways. The NER-designed 'J72' 0-6-0Ts were chosen to be decked in NER green, and were given NER crests and lining, as well as displaying their running numbers in BR Gill Sans and carrying a BR totem! They were certainly colourful. So also was the Liverpool Street station pilot, former GER 0-6-0T No 68619, which received GER ultramarine blue, fully lined out, but with BR crest on the tanksides. More striking in some people's opinion was the 'N7' 0-6-2T No 69614 which accompanied it at Liverpool Street. The 0-6-2T was painted only in BR lined black, but with much metalwork burnished. Kept brilliantly clean, in the view of the Editor it looked a picture.

Southern men were pleased that a number of the 'USA' 0-6-0Ts were set aside for departmental duties when their stint at Southampton Docks finally came to an end in the early 1960s. The authorities responded by painting the first one, which had been converted to left-hand drive for use, single manned, at Lancing carriage works, in Southern carriage stock green (the later, darker green that was *not* quite malachite!) fully lined out SR style with yellow edged in black. These engines were given diesel style, compressed sans serif numbers and the

Left:
Not only were a number of Gresley 'V2' 2-6-2s painted Brunswick green in the era of relative livery freedom which occurred in the late 1950s and early 1960s, but other variations in livery treatment also appeared. This smart 'V2' No 60813, the one with small smoke deflectors each side of a stovepipe chimney, has white painted smokebox door hinges and brackets. The white buffers suggest it had been on special duty shortly before. It is seen leaving Dundee with the 14.50 freight for Perth on 18 August 1966. *S. C. Crook*

Left:
Swindon works went through a phase of painting all steam locomotives green as they passed through the shops. Lesser engines such as BR Class 3 2-6-2Ts received no lining. No 82040 is leaving Wells on a Yatton to Witham (Cheddar Valley) train on 16 June 1962. *Michael J. Fox*

Below:
The 'Manor' class soon received lined green paint. On 9 August 1963 No 7801 *Anthony Manor* leaves Morfa Mawddach with the Pwllheli portion of the down 'Cambrian Coast Express'. *T. Boustead*

Left:
Probably one of the best known livery variations under BR was the use of full North Eastern Railway passenger livery on a few Class J72 0-6-0Ts for main station pilot duties.
No 68723 carried BR and NER crests, and poses here at Newcastle Central in 1962.
Colour-Rail/J. G. Dewing

Centre left:
The favourite station pilot at the London end was Liverpool Street's 'J69' No 68619. Stratford gave it a livery of Great Eastern dark blue, the GER crest appearing on the lower bunker side below the locomotive number.
No 68619 carries the route availability number on the tank side in front of the cab, and a full BR totem.
Colour-Rail

Bottom left:
USA 0-6-0T No DS236 poses at Lancing works shortly after delivery from Eastleigh where it had been converted to left-hand drive (for single manning) and painted in Southern Region stock green and fully lined out in Southern Railway style. Here it can be clearly seen that the totem faces left, in accordance with BR's instructions following realisation that an heraldic device should not be distorted by reversal. Unusually the livery includes the locomotive number in the compressed sans serif numerals normally used then on diesel and electric locomotives. These are repeated on the rear of the coal bunker. *Colin Boocock*

The 'Schools' class 4-4-0s received different paint treatments according to whether they were overhauled at Eastleigh or Ashford works. Eastleigh lined the cab out fully, including the rather cramped layout of the lining around the bottom of the cabside which followed the shape exactly. No 30905, in early lined black, stands at Bournemouth on 18 August 1957. *Colin Boocock*

Below:
The same engine after being painted green is seen on 19 July 1959. It carries Ashford's style of cab lining which runs off into the curve of the running plate. This view of *Tonbridge*, also taken at Bournemouth, shows the engine coupled to the self-trimming tender that had for so many years been coupled to No 30932 *Blundells*. *Colin Boocock*

Above:
Scottish Region Class 2P 4-4-0s received large size cabside numerals whereas the London Midland Region ones were given the smaller size. No 40648, a Scottish one which also sports (uniquely?) a below-centre smokebox door numberplate, was seen at Kittybrewster, Aberdeen, on 14 July 1960. *Colin Boocock*

Left:
Some works managed to paint the lining of black engines with wider lines than others did. Ashford appears to have done this on 'H' class 0-4-4T No 31500 in summer 1956. *Colin Boocock*

Below left:
Subtle white edging to the smokebox door numberplate of ex-North British 4-4-2T No 67474 adds a little brightness to BR lined black. This is the Arrochar to Craigendoran push-pull train by Loch Long in April 1959.
S. C. Crook

later BR totem. Two more were similarly painted for use at Ashford, and named *Wainwright* and *Maunsell*, and yet two more (Nos 30064 and — I believe — 30073) were also painted green for use as Eastleigh works shunters, though these last two were not in departmental stock and had their running numbers painted in normal Gill Sans style.

One other odd livery had been perpetuated throughout the Southern's reign at Brighton works, where No 377s (later DS377), a Stroudley 'Terrier' 0-6-0T, was retained in former LB&SCR 'improved engine green', actually a pale yellow which the Editor felt was most attractive!

As electrification progressed, on the 25kV ac system using overhead contact wire, it became obligatory that all locomotives be embellished with warning flashes to alert staff not to climb above a safe level. Neat, white backed red flashes with a warning message were fixed at appropriate places, usually where there were steps or ladders granting access to the upper parts of a locomotive. No exception was made — all locomotives (indeed all rolling stock) were given warning flashes no matter how unlikely it was that they would ever be routed under the wires.

The LM Region also was the instigator of the last new addition to the liveries of steam locomotives on BR. When the electrification of the West Coast main line was in progress, the later phases of the scheme had the overhead contact wire clearances reduced from the dimensions used in the earlier parts of the scheme. Some LMS design steam locomotives exceeded the safe height to work under the wire in these sections (which were mostly south of Crewe). In order to identify that these locomotives were banned from these restricted clearance lines, a broad yellow diagonal band was painted on the lower cabside, thus disfiguring, among others, 'Jubilees', 'Duchesses' and '4F' 0-6-0s. The yellow bands found their way on to former LNER locomotives including some 'A3s' and even two 'A4s'.

An unexpected use of a standard livery occurred when the ER and ScR experienced a shortage of TSOs (open second coaches) at a time (1966) when the Southern had a surplus of them. Eight Bulleid TSOs were given C3 overhauls at Eastleigh works and were repainted in fully lined-out BR maroon, the only Southern Railway-designed coaches known to have been so treated.

Left:
Liverpool Street station pilot No 68619 poses in its pseudo Great Eastern dark blue livery on 5 August 1961. *Colin Boocock*

Below left:
It was not normal practice to line out the Class 15XX 0-6-0 pannier tanks which were painted plain black as standard. No 1504 was seen lined out, however, standing at Old Oak Common on 17 November 1957.
Colin Boocock

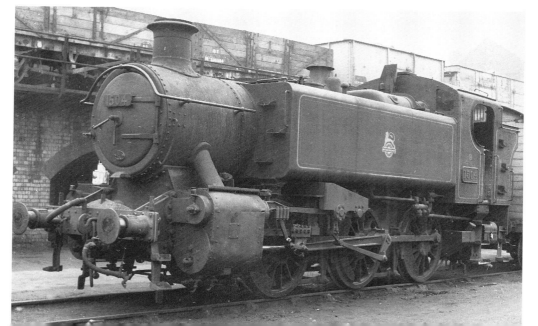

Right:
The limited space for applying numbers and totems on the three remaining Beattie 2-4-0 well tanks cramped Eastleigh's style! To get the running number on the bunker side the paint shop used compressed sans serif numerals of the style used on diesel locomotives. After its last general overhaul No 30586 was photographed at Eastleigh on 2 March 1960 when it was 86 years old. *Colin Boocock*

Centre right:
The Southern Region followed to the letter the BR instruction to paint extended power classifications to its locomotives. The Urie 'H15' rebuilds of Drummond's 'F13s' and 'E14' were classed 4P/5FA and that is how it was stencilled on the cabside of No 30335, seen at Eastleigh in 1957. And why did it have such a small totem on such a large tender? *Colin Boocock*

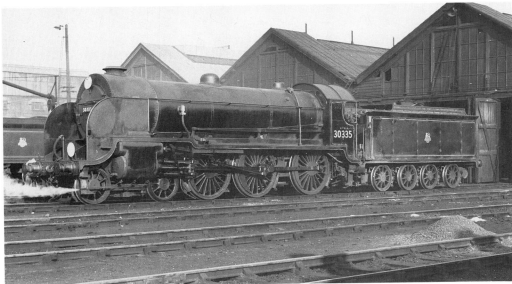

Below:
A plain black ex-GWR 'Large Prairie' 2-6-2T received little adornment. No 6129, seen at Reading on 15 March 1959, carries only the large totem, and its route disc below its cabside numberplate. Yet BR's instruction for mixed traffic locomotives was for them to be lined black! *Colin Boocock*

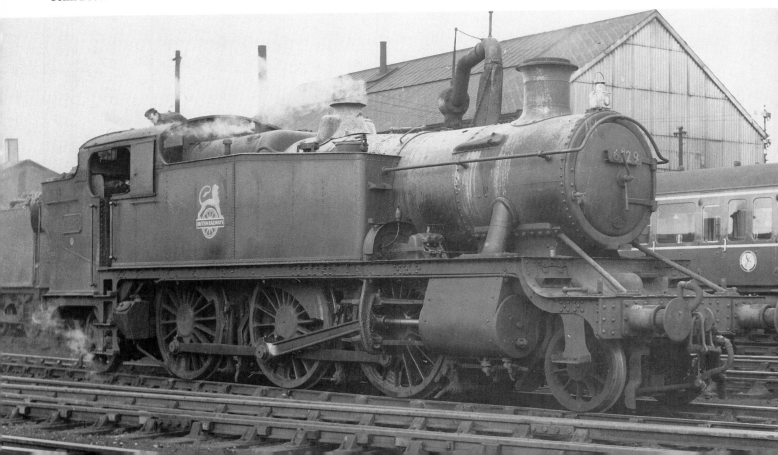

Left:
Painting stars on smokebox doors was quite a popular unofficial embellishment, but few depots went to the extent of painting the heads of smokebox door bracket bolts white as well! Bournemouth depot kept 'M7' No 30111 tarted up for its pilot duties at Bournemouth West terminus in 1955.
Colin Boocock

Centre left:
Another Scottish Region decoration went to BR standard Class 3 2-6-0 No 77019. Seen at Glasgow St Enoch station in 1956, the smokebox door hinge straps shine out in white.
Colin Boocock

Below:
To indicate that they could not work under the wires south of Crewe, many of the locomotives were marked by broad yellow diagonal bands across their cabsides. So disfigured, rebuilt 'Royal Scot' class 4-6-0 No 46152 hauls the 3.40pm from Bradford to Carlisle out of Settle on 3 April 1965.
P. F. Claxton

5. BRUSHES AND SPRAYS

During the 1960s, a major change took place in the method of painting locomotives and rolling stock. Until then, painting had been carried out by traditional methods which had been developed over 130 years of railways and stood the test of time.

The traditional method was very time-consuming and costly, but enabled a superb finish to be applied. Only now are similar standards close to being regained by the latest paint products.

The techniques were much the same for locomotives or carriages. The reader will permit me to describe them in some detail, because of their relevance to the changes which followed, which themselves brought further changes to liveries on BR in their wake.

In BR days it was normal practice not to strip off all old paint at a vehicle overhaul but to chip off any that was loose, leaving intact good, sound paintwork as a base. Bare metal areas were painted with a rust-inhibiting primer, followed by applications of stopping and filling media, usually applied by knife, the purpose of which was to fill in

Left:
Imagine painting the lining, numbering and lettering on this 2-6-4T all by hand! Before full sets of transfers were available that is how the earliest examples of the new standard BR liveries were produced. Class L1 No 67724 looks well as a result of the treatment.
E. R. Wethersett

Below left:
Two-tone liveries on carriages were also time-consuming in their application. Each colour had to be applied separately, and the lining-out done by hand. No 45341 pulls away from Morley (Low) with a Leeds to Manchester express during the 1955 footplate strike. *A. M. Ross*

Right:
While at general repairs locomotives were fully repainted, those receiving intermediate overhauls were touched up. Sometimes this was not visually satisfactory, as witness the patchwork effect on green 'Battle of Britain' 4-6-2 No 34087 in 1959. *Colin Boocock*

surface blemishes and so present a smooth surface to the paint to be applied later. Between each of these operations the surface was rubbed down, or 'flatted', with wet emery cloth. Bare filler was primed, rubbed down, and then the vehicle presented for painting. In some works, such as the locomotive works at Crewe and Doncaster and virtually all the carriage works, the preparation work was done while the vehicle overhaul was under way, and the final painting work was segregated in a separate paint shop. Other locomotive works, for example St Rollox, Eastleigh and Swindon, carried out the whole paint operation in the erecting shop as the locomotive's overhaul progressed.

A thick undercoat was usually applied as the first paint stage, its colour being suited to the main colour to be applied later. The Editor recalls that black engines usually missed out on this stage. Then the top coat was applied, all the paintwork

having been done by the traditional method using paint brushes. Good paint brushes had long bristles, enabling a useful area to be painted before refilling the brush.

After the top coat had dried, the lettering, totems and lining were applied. Transfers were used for lettering, numbers and the BR totem. Lining out a locomotive was the most skilled part of the painting work. First the route of the line had to be marked. This was done by chalking a long length of string, stretching it along where the line had to be painted, and giving the string a strong 'twang', whereupon it deposited chalk on the vehicle, marking precisely

where the line was to be. Then a special, thin and very long-bristled brush was loaded with the appropriate paint colour, and, guided by the chalk line and a hand-held hand rest, the brush was applied to the locomotive or carriage in a confident, straight pass. To watch a skilled signwriter doing this was to witness generations of acquired technique being demonstrated.

Then came a coat of gloss varnish, over the whole of the livery area, more often two coats, to give the paintwork the protection, sheen and depth which characterised a beautifully painted locomotive or carriage. Between each coat of paint or varnish the vehicle had to stand for around 24hr, so painting could not be done quickly.

At intermediate overhauls, carriages and locomotives were not usually repainted, but merely touched up where the existing paint surface was blemished, and then the whole livery area was revarnished. To the untrained eye the finished vehicle could look as if it had been repainted throughout!

Smokeboxes, running gear, frames, wheels and other non-liveried areas were usually painted base black, that is an unskilled painter would daub black paint on them without any special preparation, apart from cleaning, and no varnish.

The revolution in painting methods which came to British Railways in the mid-1960s was caused by the use of spray paint. The technique was not used on steam locomotives, to the Editor's knowledge, but it was adopted at most carriage works for coaching stock and multiple-units. The paint was of

a thicker formulation than for brush application, and it had the added advantage that it would cover very well indeed. It became possible to contemplate a livery change using one coat of spray paint! No varnish was required, the paint thickness and surface being deemed adequate for normal wear to the next repaint. This also enabled intermediate overhauls on carriages to be carried out with one-coat paint spraying, instead of applying two coats of varnish.

Spray painting of coaching stock had a number of disadvantages to balance the speeding up of application. It was necessary to mask up any areas where the paint was not supposed to go, for example the carriage windows, the roof, or another colour area in the livery. Masking was usually done by taping paper across the affected areas, which proved to be labour intensive.

The spray technique was intended to be used for the new corporate image colours which began to appear in 1965 and which are not the subject of this book. However, the ability to avoid the need to varnish at intermediate repairs prompted some works to use the method of spray painting single coats on coaches that were not listed for colour change at that time. For example, the author is aware of maroon vans, SR green multiple-units and at least one dark green GE section electric multiple unit being spray painted, the lining being omitted in all cases.

The spray technique gave rise to one change in livery style around 1965. Carriage ends were no longer to be painted black (which would have meant masking them off when the bodysides were sprayed) but could be painted the same colour as the sides, maroon or green.

In later years, because of the complication of masking off BR's two-tone colours on main line stock, many works reverted to brush application, though York and Glasgow did try pressure-fed paint rollers for a time.

Below:
Care had to be taken that preparation for repainting was carried out correctly. If a smooth surface was not prepared it was possible to get results such as this, where 'N7' 0-6-2T No 69727's prewar LNER number (2625) shows through under the new paint below the totem after a repaint at Stratford in 1958. *Colin Boocock*

Above left:
Swindon's unilateral adoption of plain unlined Brunswick green for all locomotives in the early 1960s led to this unsatisfactory appearance of 2-6-0 No 6373 in February 1962. *H. Wheeler*

Left:
When appearance was thought not to matter, such as with departmental engines, short cuts were often taken. New numerals without repainting the locomotive had been applied to this ex-Lancashire & Yorkshire Railway 0-6-0ST at Horwich works. The engine carried its former LMS number into BR departmental stock and was photographed in 1957.
Colin Boocock

Below:
Even the small size numerals and totem look cramped on diminutive Stroudley 'Terrier' 0-6-0T No 32640. The livery is, however, correct in every detail. *Colin Boocock*

6. PULLMAN STYLE

During most of the World War 2 period the Pullman Car Co's services had been suspended, apart from a few cars used by government ministers, royalty, and senior War Office officials as VIP specials (in some cases in conditions of secrecy), and the vast bulk of the fleet was stored. Grey paint was applied all over the stored cars to render them less conspicuous to enemy aircraft, while those actually running were in umber brown or LNER brown (teak shade).

When the war ended, a new Chairman, Stanley Adams, and a recently appointed General Manager, Frank Harding, quickly set about the task of reintroducing Pullman car services in Britain. The Pullman Car Co was not affected by the 1948 railway nationalisation and remained a private company operating its cars over BR tracks. Then, in 1954 the British Transport Commission gained financial control of the company. It chose, however, to leave it for several years as a separately managed entity, and through most of the period covered by this book it was identifiable by its own name, livery, coat of arms, uniforms and publicity, all of which

dated back, in essence, to the prewar days when Lord Dalziel was Chairman. The company also had its own workshops, at Preston Park, Brighton.

Work on restoring war-damaged cars was quickly put in hand, and an outstanding 1938 order for some new ones was resurrected. Within a remarkably short time the famous Pullman trains — the 'Golden Arrow', 'Brighton Belle', 'Bournemouth Belle', 'Yorkshire Pullman', 'Queen of Scots' and so on were running once again, and there was a new service, the 'Devon Belle' to Plymouth and Ilfracombe. On the Southern, Pullman cars were used for royal trains and special trains for the visits of foreign heads of state and important overseas guests. No Pullman cars operated on the London Midland Region, but they were destined to do so later, while for the first seven years after nationalisation no Pullmans ran on the Western Region.

In 1955 however, the BTC introduced the 'South Wales Pullman' service so that between 1955 and around 1960 Pullman cars operated on all Regions except the London Midland. A supplementary fare

Right:
Pullman car *Trianon* was beautifully repainted for the reintroduction of the 'Golden Arrow' service, after the war during which most Pullmans had been stored out of use painted grey. The standard livery of umber brown for body ends, doors, sides below waist and fascia boards above windows was offset by a broad cream area. Lettering was cream or gold, as was the lining out. On this example the coat of arms is nearer to the entrance door than usual to make room for the special 'Fleche D'Or' and 'Golden Arrow' inscriptions. Undergear and bogies were plain black. On this car the roof was grey. White or aluminium was used during 1948 to 1957 for the roofs of cars repainted for special duties such as Royal trains or Ascot specials.
Courtesy of the National Railway Museum, York

was charged for their use, and passengers received at-the-table service from courteous attendants.

The Pullman livery was a standard one dating back to the purchase of the British group from the American parent company in 1907. The group adopted the new colours of umber brown and cream (ivory white) that D. E. Marsh had started to use on the London, Brighton & South Coast Railway (LB&SCR) the previous year. This was a logical move because most of his cars at first ran on the LB&SCR and it made them match the handsome new locomotives that Marsh was introducing.

Slight modifications were made to the juxtaposition of the colours over the years. By 1948 the standard was:

> Umber brown bodysides, waistline and below, and fascia boards above windows. Umber brown doors and body ends. Cream window area down to waistline and up to the lower edge of the fascia boards. White roof (aluminium on the steel 'Brighton Belle' cars) and black under-gear and bogies. All decoration in gold leaf, and lettering in 'old gold' with black shading. The name 'Pullman' in elongated shaded serif letters was on the umber fascia boards. Two coats of arms were on the lower umber bodysides, one adjacent to each end door. A central panel on the lower umber area carried the name or number of the car

in old gold, black shaded Roman characters. All brasswork for door handles, grab rails and so forth was kept highly polished. On the 'Brighton Belle' EMU Pullman sets, the driving ends were in umber brown, lined in gold and the Pullman coat of arms was carried centrally below the headcode panel. Bufferbeams were normally painted black, but red was reported to have been used during BR days on at least one 'Brighton Belle' set.

The Pullman cars ran in complete train formations on BR, or as individual vehicles marshalled into trains of ordinary BR stock according to operating needs. It should be recorded that most Pullman cars operating in the 1948-67 period were of prewar origin and in some cases were wooden bodied. New cars were supplied for use on the East Coast main line by Cravens in the late 1950s, with bodies based on BR's Mk 1 coach but with inward opening access doors.

There were subtle changes to the standard Pullman livery from time to time. From photographs in the book *Bournemouth & Southampton Steam 1947-1967* (Ian Allan, 1985) in

the chapter 'Pullman Perfection', the Editor has noted that the colour of the bodyside upper panels between the passenger section and the brake van doors was cream on most brake-end vehicles early in BR days, but this area was painted all-over umber in later years, after around 1957. Also, the coat of arms was changed from the original to a wider, flatter version of the same thing around 1960.

Another change, this time in lettering, which the Editor cannot accurately date but which may have been around 1950, was to the inscription on

Left:
There are those who believe that the layout of the BR 1956 totem owed something to Mr Bulleid's splendid nameplates for his 'Merchant Navy' class 4-6-2s! The nameplate of No 35027 *Port Line,* **seen here in its restored condition, has black backing and displays the flag of the Port Line shipping fleet on the enamel disc in the centre.**
Colin Boocock

Left:
While the Isle of Wight locomotives never carried smokebox door numberplates, they did retain their Southern Railway bunker numberplates with their W prefixes. *Merstone* **shows its red-backed numberplate and its tank side nameplate, also backed in red, while running round its train at Cowes.** *Ian Allan Library*

Below:
No 56025 is a smart-looking little 'pug', but what is it doing in fully lined out black passenger/mixed traffic style? Scotland has also honoured it with red coupling and connecting rods and polished metalwork, including a star on the smokebox door. It was seen at St Rollox works in June 1957.
Colour-Rail/P. W. Gray

The standard BR headboard style followed closely that of the former LNER, but the boards were cast in aluminium alloy. No 60027 *Merlin*, seen ready to leave Edinburgh with the non-stop 'Elizabethan' to King's Cross on 15 July 1960, has a blue-painted headboard on display. *Colin Boocock*

8. PRE-GROUPING REVIVAL

Above:
**The return of the Great Western 4-4-0 No 3440 *City of Truro*
to regular traffic, to make it available for the occasional
special working, delighted enthusiasts and public alike.
The splendid apparition is seen pausing at Eastleigh while
working a train from Newbury to Southampton Terminus
in April 1957. The livery is said to be 1903 style. Note how
much brighter the background carmine red coaches appear
than is generally remembered today.** *Colour-Rail*

Left:
**The Caledonian single 4-2-2 No 123, known as the 'royal
pilot' engine because of its former duty to precede royal
specials at a discreet distance for security reasons, was a
surprise restoration to traffic in view of its limited haulage
ability. It did look nice in Caledonian blue, and once visited
the Bluebell Railway where it is seen here.** *G. Grigs*

Above right:
**A Class D40 4-4-0 poses in its restored condition as Great
North of Scotland Railway No 49 *Gordon Highlander* in
Kittybrewster shed, Aberdeen, in summer 1960.**
Colin Boocock

Right:
**Regularly used for railtours because of its useful power was
North British 4-4-0 No 256 *Glen Douglas*. Here it is piloting
a former NBR 0-6-0 on an enthusiasts' special in the
Berwickshire border country.** *Colin Boocock*

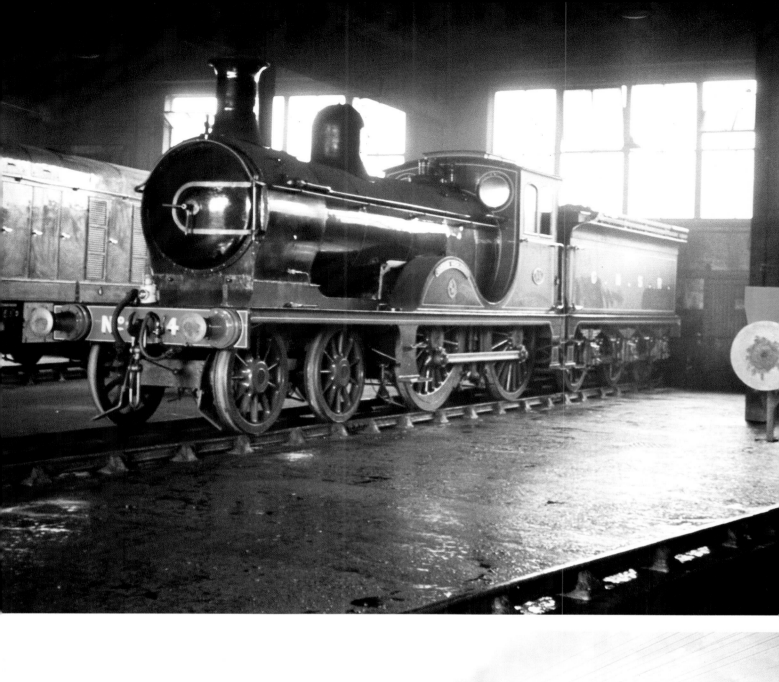

One evening in 1957 at Eastleigh the Editor was chatting to a friend, standing near the SR main line when a train for the Didcot, Newbury & Southampton line approached. Much to the astonishment of the two young men the train was headed, not by the expected Collett 0-6-0, but by the 4-4-0 No 3440 *City of Truro*, last known to have been resident in York railway museum. That the engine was in 1903 livery was clear: Brunswick green with reddish-brown valances and outside frames, fully lined out almost to excess, with a very fussy version of a GWR monogram on the tender. The effect was startling!

City of Truro had indeed been brought out of retirement (where it had posed in later GWR livery) and put into running order. This was on the grounds that it was available for working special trains provided it also had work to do when not so required, thus enabling the cost of restoration to working order to be recovered.

Other Regions followed this trend with enthusiasm. The LM Region offered its compound 4-4-0 No 1000, straight from revenue traffic, and painted it in Midland red with the number in large numerals on the tender.

The Scottish did much better. They brought two engines out of retirement, the Caledonian 4-2-2 No 123 and the Highland Railway 'Jones Goods' 4-6-0 No 103. The liveries of these two were thought to be the authentic Caledonian and Highland colours respectively, but many believed the use of Stroudley yellow on the 4-6-0 was inappropriate, however nice it looked (Editor)! Scotland also restored two engines out of revenue traffic, the Great North of Scotland Railway 4-4-0 *Gordon*

Highlander and the North British Railway No 256 *Glen Douglas*, also in pregrouping liveries.

On the Southern Region a proposal was made to paint a South Eastern & Chatham Railway 'L' class 4-4-0 in SE&CR grey, and a 'T9' in London & South Western Railway (LSWR) green. Only the latter was authorised, and No 120 appeared, to take up duties from Eastleigh shed. This 'T9' had not been superheated until after the formation of the Southern Railway and so the perfectionists complained that it should not be in LSWR green; others said that there was too much white in the green. However, No 120 did look good, and few were so churlish as to turn down the opportunity of seeing it when it turned out on specials.

All these engines ran in regular traffic in order to justify their restoration to working order, though the Editor does not recall the Midland compound being so used.

The 'T9', the GNSR 4-4-0 and *Glen Douglas* would quite likely have been scrapped had this extended and unexpected lease of life not been granted.

Readers may ask what place these preserved engines have in a book about railway liveries on British Railways. As most were locomotives used in everyday traffic for a period in their pregrouping colours, their liveries were for a time a part (if a very small one!) of the BR scene.

Below:
Several old locomotives were restored for use on special trains in the 1960s provided they could also continue to work normal services. The LSWR green used on Class T9 4-4-0 No 120 was said to be too white according to 'those who knew', though the paint shop at Eastleigh works had actually followed the formula quoted by the manufacturers. *A. J. Lambert*

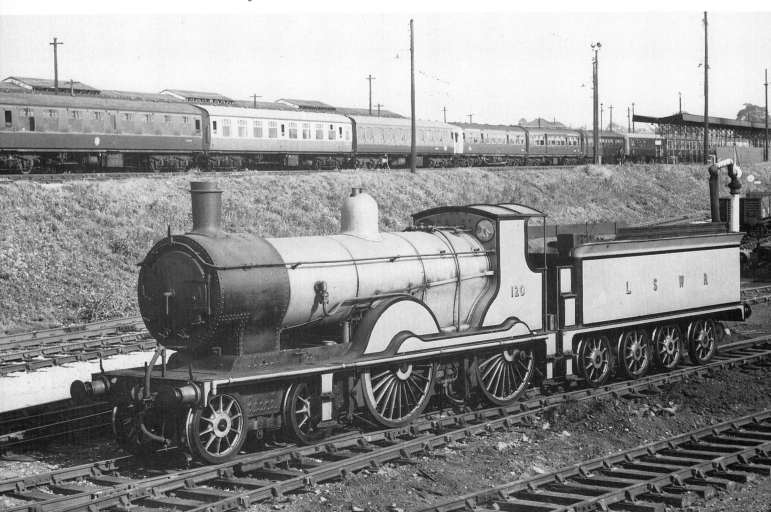

Above:
Scotland's No 256 *Glen Douglas* was painted a shade of green nearing mid-brown and was given complex North British lining out. The effect was striking, as seen here on the locomotive as it stands at St Boswell's on 9 July 1961.
Colin Boocock

Below:
Midland Compound 4-4-0 No 1000 was painted crimson lake lined out in straw edged in black. Its superb finish is evident from this view as its backs into Leeds City to couple to a special working in 1961. *Colin Boocock*

Above:
The immaculate appearance of Midland compound 4-4-0 No 1000 in early LMS crimson lake colour made it a firm favourite for special trains. No 1000 was also a brilliant performer. Here it is posing at Rugby Central station in September 1960.
Colour-Rail/K. C. H. Fairey

Right:
The most colourful restored running steam locomotive in the late 1950s was undoubtedly the Highland 'Jones Goods' 4-6-0. No 103 is seen near Balnacra on the Kyle line in 1959.
Colour-Rail

APPENDIX 1: 1949 LIVERY DETAILS

Above:
The earliest version of full BRITISH RAILWAYS lettering on tenders and tank sides on the Western Region used standard GWR shaded lettering, applied by hand. *Colin Boocock*

Left:
The famous lion-over-wheel emblem appeared in 1949. This photograph shows the style and colouring. The lining of this tender is red, cream and grey.
Colin Boocock

Steam Locomotives

a) Blue or Green Locomotives:

The colour is applied to boiler and firebox lagging plates, cab front and cabsides, tendersides and rear, side valances and splashers. Cylinder covers are black, with double white or orange lining. Otherwise, all parts below the footplate and platform angles are black and unlined; this applies particularly to wheels and axle ends which may previously have been painted differently. The motion remains bright metal. The exposed parts on tender tops and cab roofs are black. The tender rear is unlined as is the cab front. Side valances are edged in black and white (blue locomotives) or black and orange (green locomotives), except that on ex-GWR locomotives the side valances are unlined black (blue locomotives) or unlined green.

The lining on cab and tendersides is black with the white or orange lines painted either side. The white or orange lines are spaced from the black line (see Fig 1). Boiler lagging bands are painted black with the edges lined in white or orange. The lining on side valances has the black line on the lower edge, with the white or orange line immediately adjoining. On wheel splashers the black line is on the outer edge with the white or orange line adjoining on the inside. In all the above cases, white lining is only used on blue locomotives, and orange lining on green locomotives.

All parts below the tender are black and unlined. This applies particularly to the wheels, frames, and so on which may previously have been painted otherwise.

b) Lined Black Locomotives:

Lining is in the same positions as on coloured locomotives, otherwise everything is plain black. The lining on cab and tendersides is painted with the broad grey line on the outside, edged with the narrow cream band inside. The red line is further inside, spaced away from the cream one. On the valances, the lining is the same, with the grey line at the bottom edge of the valance. Boiler lagging bands are edged with two red lines, as are the cylinder cover bands.

c) All Other Steam Locomotives:

Plain black with no lining or other livery features, except as below.

d) Other Details:

All lettering and numerals are Gill Sans in cream, edged with a narrow black band. Nameplates are backed in black, except on lined black locomotives (and on blue SR locomotives) where red nameplate back colour can be used. Cabside numberplates (WR) are backed in black, except they can be red on lined black locomotives. All lettering is capitals (upper case) only.

Buffer beams, front and rear, are vermilion red. Smokeboxes and smokebox doors are plain black on all locomotives. Lettering on cast iron plates is white on black background.

Power class codes appear in small lettering above the cabside numbers.

The BR lion-over-wheel totem appears centrally on the tender or tankside. There are alternative sizes of totem depending on the space available to affix them. There are also left-facing and right-facing versions, so that the lion can be fixed always to face the direction of forward movement of the locomotive.

Coaching Stock

The cream panel is the full height of the window, plus an inch above and below. Above and below the cream panel run the black and gold lines, the former adjacent to the cream panel. The black line is ¾in and the gold ⅜in in width. All other areas of the bodysides are carmine red. Vehicle ends are black, as is everything below the body panels, including underframe, bogies, battery boxes and brake gear. (There was thus no set distance above rail level for the joins between the two main livery colours on the bodysides, and a train of vehicles of mixed designs, as occurred frequently on the WR and ER, presented a somewhat untidy appearance [Editor].)

For all other vehicles, that is suburban and local carriages, parcels vans, and so on, the livery is carmine red on the sides with the gold and black lining in the same dimensions and positions.

In all cases, carriage roofs are light grey and the guttering or cornice black. (An oddity was the painting of the former GWR diesel railcars in carmine and cream livery for a few years, the parcels cars being all-carmine as with locomotive-hauled stock. These were repainted in DMU green nearer the end of their lifespan.)

Lettering on all Passenger Rolling Stock

The fleet number of each coach is in 4in figures with prefix letter indicating the former owning company where necessary. (This was changed in 1951 to a suffix, the prefix afterwards being used to denote the Region to which the vehicle was allocated.) The top of the figures is 6in below the bottom of the waistline, or 7in below the bottom of the windows where no waistline exists; alternatively it may be on the inside of panelling where this is present on older stock. The number is placed immediately to the right of the door at the extreme left of the vehicle as seen from the exterior. (This was quickly changed to the extreme right-hand end of the vehicle.) Brake vans and other vehicles conform with the foregoing as nearly as possible.

a) Restaurant and Buffet Cars, Sleeping Cars:

The vehicle description (eg: RESTAURANT CAR) is in 6in letters, placed centrally along the side of the vehicle. The tops of the letters are 6in below the bottom of the waistline, or as near as possible to this on the older types of vehicle.

b) First-Class Compartments:
Indicated by a figure 1 painted to style on the door, and by a white-on-blue totem sticker lettered FIRST on windows.

c) Other Lettering Details:
Painted or transferred lettering on solebars for date of examination, loading directions etc is in 3in letters and figures for loading directions and 1½in for all other matters including loading directions on bodysides. The cast letters and plates for the tare weight and date and place of building remain as previously for the time being on vehicles to designs by the previous companies, except that the initials of the former company, if shown, are omitted, ie painted over in black.

NB As already mentioned, the official description for lettering and numbers was for them to be in gold, or golden yellow. In practice, the transfers supplied were in a creamy-yellow shade, with fine black outline. All lining was done by hand.

Figs 1 & 2 (*Right*) **Dimensions for lining out a steam locomotive cabside, with numeral details, as prescribed in 1949. Dimensions of the three forms of lining out of footplate angles and other areas (except boilers).**

Fig 3 (*Below*) **This lozenge style emblem was the Railway Executive's official BRITISH RAILWAYS device, but was displaced for use on locomotives by the BTC lion-over-wheel totem.**

Fig 4 (*Bottom*) **General details of lettering for covered wagons.**

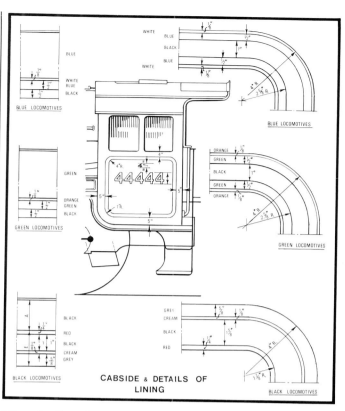

CABSIDE & DETAILS OF LINING

Freight Stock

Lettering Details: All lettering is in white Gill Sans medium type except for International markings on containers. (The Tare, Charge and Capacité figures are the metric equivalents of Tare, Load, and Capacity figures on International containers.)

All wagons carry the following prefixes to their numbers:

B for new wagons and for ex-MoT and MWT 16T mineral wagons

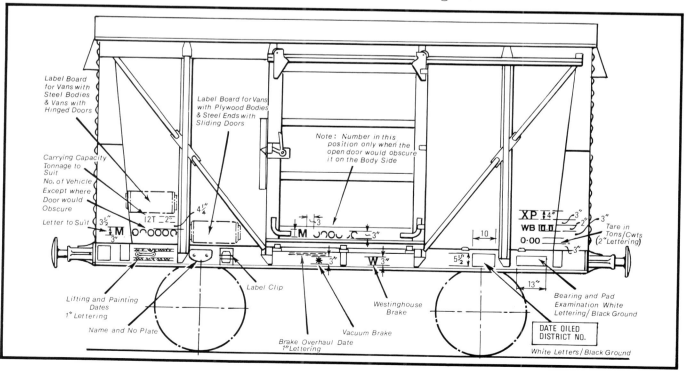

Cylinder covers on green locomotives were painted black, lined in orange. On BR Standard locomotives and rebuilt Bulleid Pacifics only, the running plate valances, being broader than in previous practice, were lined out with a continuous orange line. *Colin Boocock*

Left:
This close-up of preserved 4-6-2 No 34105 (on the Mid-Hants Railway) shows the different ways in which orange and black lining was applied to BR locomotives with Brunswick green livery. The parallel lines on the air-smoothed casings of Bulleid Pacifics (see the left of the photograph) were broad black lines edged in orange (the same as on the vertical boiler lagging bands on other green locomotives), whereas on the cabs of such Bulleid engines that had modified tenders the same style was used as on all other locomotives' cabs and tenders, namely the orange lines were spaced discreetly away from the black. Note the locomotive number transfer embodies black edging to the cream numerals. *Colin Boocock*

Left:
Former GWR 'Small Prairie' 2-6-2T No 4566 on the Severn Valley Railway displays lining within its cabside numberplate, and (correctly) no lining on the valance below the running plate. The yellow disc painted above the numberplate is the Western Region route code and the locomotive is of power class C. *Colin Boocock*

Right:
The Pullman crest appeared in a 'stretched' version around 1960, as seen here. On earlier versions, while the same shield was used, the lions were upright and the whole crest occupied considerably less width. *Courtesy of the National Railway Museum, York*

Below left:
The 1956 totem embodied the demi-lion rampant from the BTC official heraldic crest. Thus convention required that the lion always had to face left.
Colin Boocock

Below:
For coaching stock the same lion-over-crown emblem was placed inside a circular device which, to the Editor, was aesthetically quite pleasing. This one is on a BR Mk 1 vehicle painted chocolate and cream.
Colin Boocock

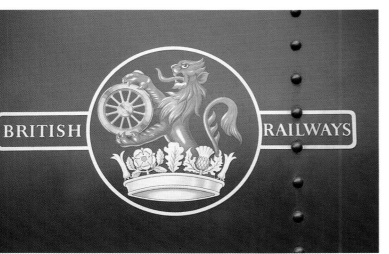

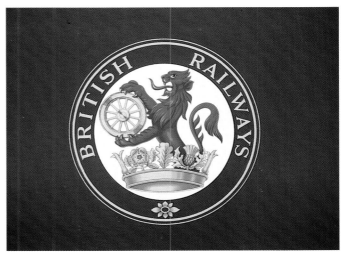

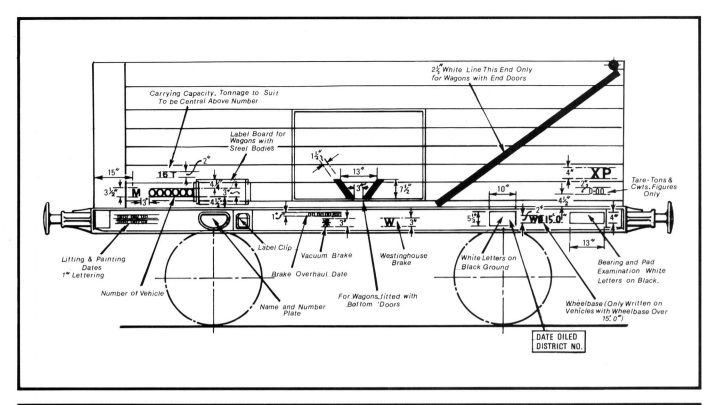

Carrying Capacity. Tonnage to Suit
To be Central Above Number

2½" White Line This End Only
for Wagons with End Doors

Label Board for
Wagons with
Steel Bodies

15" 16 T 2"

3½" M 000000 3"

1½"

13"

3" 7½"

10"

4" XP
2"
0·00

Tare· Tons &
Cwts. Figures
Only

1" 3"

W 3"

5½" W B 15·0 2"

13" 4"

Lifting & Painting
Dates
1" Lettering

Label Clip

Vacuum Brake

Westinghouse
Brake

White Letters on
Black Ground

Bearing and Pad
Examination White
Letters on Black.

Number of Vehicle

Brake Overhaul Date

Name and Number
Plate

For Wagons fitted with
Bottom 'Doors

Wheelbase (Only Written on
Vehicles with Wheelbase Over
15'. 0")

DATE OILED
DISTRICT NO.

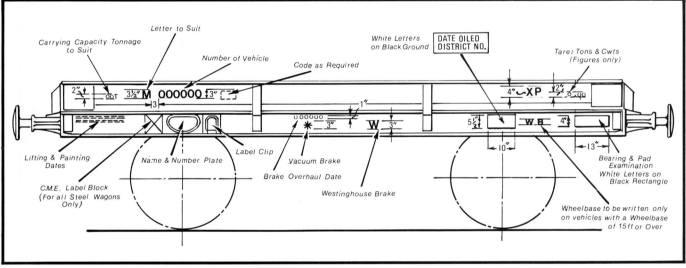

Carrying Capacity Tonnage
to Suit

Letter to Suit

Number of Vehicle

Code as Required

White Letters
on Black Ground

DATE OILED
DISTRICT NO.

Tare: Tons & Cwts
(Figures only)

2" 00 T 3½" M 000000 3"

3

1"

0·00000 3"

W 3"

5½" W B 4"

4" XP 2"
0·00

10"

13"

Lifting & Painting
Dates

Name & Number Plate

Label Clip

Vacuum Brake

Brake Overhaul Date

Westinghouse Brake

Bearing & Pad
Examination
White Letters on
Black Rectangle

C.M.E. Label Block
(For all Steel Wagons
Only)

Wheelbase to be written only
on vehicles with a Wheelbase
of 15ft or Over

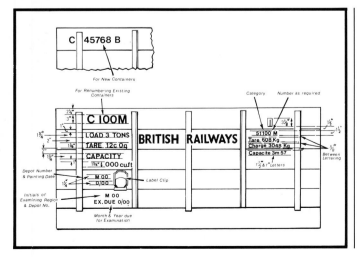

C | 45768 B

For New Containers

For Renumbering Existing
Containers

C 100M

LOAD 3 TONS

TARE 12c 0q

CAPACITY
1¾" 000 cuft

BRITISH RAILWAYS

Category

Number as required

51100 M
Tare 608 Kg
Charge 3048 Kg
Capacite 3m 57

M 00
0/00

Label Clip

M 00
EX.DUE 0/00

Depot Number
& Painting Date

Initials of
Examining Region
& Depot No.

Month & Year due
for Examination

Fig 5 (top) **General livery details of standard open wagons.**

Fig 6 (above) **Details of a typical flat one-plank wagon.**

E for ex-LNER types
M for ex-LMS types
S for ex-SR types
W for ex-GWR types
P for ex-private owner wagons

Service vehicles carry an additional D prefix (for Departmental), eg DM000000 etc.

All containers carry numbers with a prefix C, and use the above-mentioned letters as suffixes.

The power brake symbol XP and wheelbase markings are applied as required.

Fig 7 (left) **Lettering for containers.**

APPENDIX 2: FORMER GWR POWER GROUPS AND ROUTE CODES

While readers may be well familiar with the BR power classifications '7P', '4F' etc), the former GWR codes may need explanation, so they are outlined here. The power groups were displayed on the locomotives by a letter within the route availability colour disc, usually above the cabside numberplate. The codes were as follows:

Tractive effort not exceeding (lb)	Group letter
16,500	Ungrouped
18,500	A
20,500	B
25,000	C
33,000	D
38,000	E
above 38,000	Special

The colours of the route restriction discs were as follows:

Axleload	Route colour
Up to 14tons	Uncoloured
Up to 16tons	Yellow
Up to 17tons 12cwt	Blue
Over 17tons 12cwt	Red
'King' class only	Double red

Although in BR days the Western Region was included in the BR standard scheme for power groups by numbers and letters (eg '8P') it continued to use the former GWR scheme. In fact, only a few WR engines, other than BR standard types, carried the BR notation, although the reverse applied, and some former LMS and BR Standard engines allocated to the Western actually carried the former GWR route discs!

Above right:
The cabside of rebuilt 'Battle of Britain' 4-6-2 No 34087 *145 Squadron* carries the extended power code over the running number. The yellow triangle below the number denotes that full briquette water treatment is in operation. *M. J. Esau*

Right:
On the cabside of 'Hall' class 4-6-0 No 6990 *Witherslack Hall*, above the numberplate, is the red disc route availability code, embodying the former GWR power code D. The X immediately above the numberplate denotes a locomotive able to haul greater loads than normally specified for this class. *J. R. Carter*

This evocative shot of Class N15 0-6-2T No 69163 banking the 'Queen of Scots' Pullman out of Glasgow Queen Street station contains a surprising amount of livery information from 1961!

The locomotive carries the early (incorrect) right-facing version of the 1956 totem, and two electrification flashes on the back of the bunker. The last Pullman carriage has the 1960 version of the Pullman crest. Beyond the Pullman brake coach, the train consists of new Cravens Pullman coaches on which the livery lines are at different heights to the last coach, a feature repeated elsewhere on BR when carriages of different designs were mixed in the same train. On this train the name is displayed only on a bodyside board above the brakevan. *Colour-Rail/M. Mensing*